In Mother Teresa's House: A Hospice Nurse in the Slums of Calcutta

In Mother Teresa's House: A Hospice Nurse in the Slums of Calcutta

Rosemary Dew

2006

In Mother Teresa's House: A Hospice Nurse in the Slums of Calcutta

TABLE OF CONTENTS

"The world is like the impression left by the telling of a story."
Yogavasistha, 2.3.eleven

"We must live life beautifully..."
Mother Teresa, Nobel Lecture

Please note that I have changed names and certain descriptive information relating to patients and others to disguise their identities. Also, my medical conclusions reflect my thought processes at the time and are not to be taken as medical advice.

ACKNOWLEDGMENTS

I would like to thank the many people who helped me in compiling this book. Among them are: Bess Means, Jill Pflug, Eric Washburn, Phyllis Pate, Edna Newell, Ian Dew, John Paine, John Talbot, Jane Turner, Jane Nefores-Williams, Steve Minnegrode, Kendra Harvey, Theresa Foley, Pat Zaccari, Carolyn Milton, Myra Molony, Phillis Wong, Mila Little, Jason Pitelli, and Cheryl Pellerin. Your comments and encouragement kept me going and improved the quality of my work. Of course, there would have been nothing to write without the Missionaries of Charity, as well as their volunteers and patients.

MISSIONARIES OF CHARITY
54A, A.J.C. BOSE ROAD,
CALCUTTA-700014
21st May, 02

Dear Rosemary,

Thank you very much for your letter. You are welcome to share in our humble works of love for the poorest of the poor.

Come with a heart to love and hands to serve Jesus in the crippled, the abandoned, the sick and the dying in any one of our centres. Volunteers find their own accommodation and pay for all their expenses - therefore I enclose for your information a list of hotels. You can put up at one of these till you find a more suitable place. You can meet me at the above address which is opposite Bamboo Villa Income Tax Office at 7·00 am or 3·00 p.m. daily except Thursday and Sunday.

Regarding your Visa - you can come on a tourist visa and of course you would be expected to tour. When you arrive it is best if you take a prepaid taxi from the airport to the hotel.

God loves you. He will reward your generous desire to serve Him in His little ones - the poor.

Sorry Rosemary for the long delay in responding to your letter. You will be most welcome anytime.

God bless you,

Sr. Nirmala Maria m.c.

To my darling husband, who understands that a month of humanitarian work is more valuable than a month of pay;

To the Missionaries of Charity, who understand that the little gifts are the greatest by far;

And to my children, who taught me to live beautifully.

WHY?

Soren Kierkegaard said, "Life is lived forward but only understood backwards." I'm still waiting to understand the lessons of Calcutta, but perhaps answers are too much to ask of an ancient civilization that doles out magnificence and horror by accident of birth. I never thought that nursing the poorest of India's poor would be easy; I just didn't think it would be so hard.

I'm a Lutheran, not a Catholic; a nurse, not a missionary; but that has little bearing on how I think of my time at Mother Teresa's. What stands out above all else is my admiration for her Missionaries of Charity and those who volunteer to work with them. The MCs, as Mother Teresa called them, are women and men who cheerfully dedicate their lives to serving the world's poor. Using donated money, they've set up over six hundred homes in more than a hundred countries to care for needy children and adults. Volunteers of all faiths travel at their own expense from across the globe to serve in whatever way they can. They come for many reasons—one volunteer missed his train two years ago, dropped by to see what Mother's homes were like, and never left.

I journeyed to India at a time when my life's little problems had become too big. In 2002, while working as a certified hospice and palliative care nurse, I wrote the MCs about volunteering at *Nirmal Hriday*, Mother Teresa's first House for Sick and Dying Destitutes. Sister Nirmala, Mother Teresa's successor, responded about six months later with an open invitation: I'd be welcome whenever I could get there. But by that time, I was growing disenchanted with nursing as a full-time profession. It had become an endless cycle of recording data from machines and carrying out tasks that made patients a second priority. Then, on September 11, 2001, I watched from a patient's room at the National Institutes of Health as smoke rose from the Pentagon. My previous careers—thirteen years as an FBI agent with counterintelligence and counterterrorism specialties and ten years of similar work as a consultant to the Department of Defense—had prepared me for the war on terror. I wanted to do my part.

As luck would have it, I landed a wonderful job at a Department of Defense training academy, where I hoped to contribute to military force protection. In so doing, I left the world where you make a difference one life at a time and took a job that has broader impact on America.

So Sister Nirmala's letter remained in my bedside stand, but nursing, though pushed into the background of my life, never left my blood. After a year I began to seek new avenues to use the medical knowledge I'd worked so hard to attain. Commuting over one hundred miles every day from Northern Virginia to Johns Hopkins in Baltimore, I had graduated with a B.S. in nursing after only thirteen months. If it was not to be my life's work, I wanted at least to use the skills—the gifts I'd been given—for something good.

Every once in a while, I pulled out Sister Nirmala's letter and toyed with the idea of going to Calcutta, more properly known as Kolkata. But the time and money required had never materialized. Finally, during the winter of 2003, my husband and I discussed the possibilities. The dreams became plans, and on April 1, 2004, I left the United States bound for Kolkata.

I had traveled extensively throughout my more than fifty years of life, and my Bohemian approach to this trip was to make two nights' reservations in a fine hotel and figure out the rest by day three. After all, Sister Nirmala's letter said I would be welcome whenever I could get there, and she'd given me a list of places where I might stay, so I had a starting point.

Kolkata isn't a place to spend a few days. The city and its culture are overwhelming—far too much to take in quickly. You'd leave having glimpsed some interesting sights, but mostly feeling glad to escape its turbulence. Still, amidst the chaos of human striving, Kolkata is a beautiful place with friendly people. Part of the charm is that it's a *pentimento*—a term in art meaning the artist covered one work with another, but with time and wear, the original intent has peeked through. This is the way the beauty of Kolkata emerges from its jam-packed warrens and grime-caked streets—slowly, over time.

In preparation for my trip, I went to mass at the Missionaries of Charity's Gift of Peace convent in Washington, D.C. This AIDS and homeless hospice near Catholic University is over an hour from my rural Maryland home, but not a bad trip before seven o'clock on a Saturday morning.

I felt uneasy not knowing anyone and not being Catholic, although half of my family is. Nonetheless, the Lutheran liturgy has not strayed far from its Catholic root, so I can usually follow the service. But this mass was different from the start. I entered the chapel and found barefooted, sari-clad nuns sitting on the floor chanting prayers I'd never heard. The hymns were also new to me, and the passing of the peace was done with the Indian *namaskar*, a slight bow with the palms placed together and fingers straight—similar to the way I held mine when I prayed as a child. Beyond that, the sisters' voices were sweet and youthful, their accents light and pleasing to the ear. I was intrigued that I couldn't distinguish one from another when they sang or said mass.

At breakfast, former Kolkata volunteers gave me advice on what to take: lice shampoo and modest clothing headed the list. After a meal of bread, bananas, and hot tea, it was time to work. I volunteered for the cleaning crew. First, I bleached the kitchen table and chairs, then the floor. Next, I reported to the laundry, where I joined four sisters and another volunteer washing sheets and clothing by hand. The bleach stung my eyes and made my head hurt a bit, but as a nurse I'd tackled sterner tasks, so I persevered, reminding myself that some things in life are just to be gotten through.

My thick protective gloves proved to be a liability, because when water spilled over their sides, the gloves held it next to my skin. Plus, wringing wet clothes by hand was more physically taxing than I'd imagined. The thought crossed my mind that my forearms would look like Popeye's after a month of washing sheets in Kolkata.

Throughout the chores, the sisters prayed aloud, but when there was a chance, I chatted with them. Their kindly demeanor comforted me, and they spoke of Kolkata fondly and with longing. Also, everyone smiled as they worked. One tenets of the sisters' philosophy is cheerfulness, and the walls of the hospice were plastered with Mother Teresa's sayings about turning away anger with smiles and service to the poor.

"...let us always meet each other with a smile, for the smile is the beginning of love, and once we begin to love each other, naturally we want to do something."

"I want you to find the poor here, right in your own home first. And begin love there."

Before I left, I was given a Mother Teresa medal, which I added to the Miraculous Medal that I've worn around my neck since a hospice patient's family introduced me to Saint Katherine Labouré years ago. Saint Katherine found joy in accomplishing the small labors of the hand that are necessary to care for others but are so often devalued—or dreaded—by the rest of us. In the 1820s, she left her home in the French countryside and joined the Daughters of Charity, who ran a hospice. Ten years later, the Virgin Mary spoke to her in three visions, telling her to have the Miraculous Medal struck.

Mother Teresa loved Miraculous Medals. She gave them away everywhere she went, kissing them first, then bestowing the gift with open hands. I wear the medal to remind me of the ideal of taking joy in the lowly but vital tasks of life and also to remind me that caring for others is a privilege.

In the meantime, my plans for the trip gathered steam. My travel agent found me an historic, five-star hotel called the Oberoi Grand, where I would spend the first two nights in Kolkata. I wanted to sleep in peace and get my bearings before I set off in the midst of the hot season to face the challenges that lay ahead. I decided to stay at the Oberoi for my last two nights in India as well. After all, this was my vacation, and I'd have to go back to work within a few days of returning to the United States.

I also received the requisite shots for traveling to a part of the world so different from my own. In my cubicle at work hung a card that said: "Rosemary Dew: You are due for your third rabies vaccine." I thought it might make people approach me with more care. Sadly, no one noticed my little joke. Of course, the joke was on me when, in the middle of my trip, I learned that the vaccine I'd received was recalled because it contained live virus. Fortunately, I suffered no ill effects.

I withstood most of the vaccinations with only mild discomfort. The oral typhoid made me queasy, and the multiple injections—sometimes five per session—made my arms swollen and tender. I also endured a couple of nights of chills that were so bad I dropped the pills I was trying to raise to my mouth. I think the culprit was the Japanese encephalitis booster, which can be brutal; but I'd had several injections at once, so I'm not sure which one caused it. I'm just glad I didn't have anaphylactic shock, another potential side effect of the Japanese encephalitis serum, which causes your throat to swell shut so you die from asphyxiation.

The only other negative was something the nurse who gave me the shots said. We were talking about dengue fever, which is caused by day-biting mosquitoes. Dengue is an *arbovirus*, which is the same family as yellow and Rift Valley fevers. Dengue comes in two varieties. This infection can either be terrible or so light that you hardly notice you've been ill. One type causes high fever and headache, along with muscle and joint pain, and can go away on its own. The second, dengue hemorrhagic fever, is much more severe. It spawns massive internal bleeding that leads to shock and death. Anyway, the nurse was trying to comfort me when she said the hemorrhagic form doesn't usually occur until the second infection. I guess it's two bites and you're out.

In the midst of all this, a friend asked me "why on earth" I wanted to go to Kolkata, and I couldn't come up with a satisfactory answer. There were many reasons. To an extent it was moral commitment, but there were too many things that held me in my world of luxury to claim compassion for the poor as the driving force. And for quite some time I'd wanted to experience Mother Teresa's work—it's sort of ultimate hospice. I also wanted to understand the woman who became "the Saint of the Gutters" and to be a part of the life and people she left behind when she died in 1997.

A more practical reason was that I needed to put in some nursing hours so I could keep my license current. Of course, I could do that nearer home. I couldn't say that Kolkata held a fascination for me, but one attraction was that the adventure of striking out for India without firm plans or structure reminded me of being a college student in 1970, when I was about to embark upon a junior-year-abroad program in Zagreb, Croatia. Now at the age of fifty-three, an adventure like that sounded good, but not good enough for me to abandon my family and take a month's leave without pay.

The simplest explanation I can come up with is a Milton Berle quote:

"If opportunity doesn't knock, build a door." Maybe that's what I was trying to do.

I also know I wanted to shake my life out of the rut it had settled into, to change my focus from meager problems. A prime example happened just before I left the United States. I spent the entire day trying to print a document to be sent downtown. The computer couldn't find the printer, and when it did, it appeared to be spooling but wasn't. Formatting changed inexplicably, and after seven hours I'd managed to print thirty-two of the forty pages. I didn't eat lunch or take breaks, and I spent the last three hours on the verge of tears. I had to wonder what perspective Kolkata would bring to bear on mishaps like this.

Hints of the wonderment to come occurred that same day. Jane Turner, a friend from the FBI, had sent me the most beautiful rosary I have ever seen. I didn't know how to pray the rosary, so I printed some instructions from the Internet. For the rest of the evening, I pondered the meaning of the prayers and the mysterious beauty of this string of iridescent crystal beads that seemed to be of different colors as I rolled them back and forth in the light.

I wondered what it would be like to live among nuns, women so sure of their paths that they could dedicate their lives to God alone. I'm a Christian, but to me Christianity is more of a journey than an endpoint. I respect other faiths and enjoy attending churches that are not my own. As a hospice nurse, I've participated in the dying rituals of Buddhists, Jews, Muslims, and Hindus, and have found something comforting in each of them.

I believe in God and feel his presence, but I am intrigued by John 10: 16: "Other sheep I have, which are not of this fold: them also I must bring, and they shall hear my voice; and there shall be one fold, and one shepherd." Since He sought the rest of the world, how do I know he didn't reach them? He appeared to us in a form we could understand—why not to others within the context of their cultures?

I have a degree in Slavic languages and, as a linguist, I've wondered about the translations of religious documents, since I know that languages don't allow word-for-word rendering. Think about the word "love," for example. It has four letters, one syllable, and it's not a compound word, yet several meanings come to mind. Also, time changes language in profound ways. How many English speakers can read Chaucer as easily as their local newspapers? Consider the first four lines of *Canterbury Tales*:

Whan that aprill with his shoures soote
The droghte of march hath perced to the roote,
And bathed every veyne in swich licour
Of which vertu engendred is the flour...

Translators must choose from various meanings for words, based upon their understanding of the language at the time it was written. I believe that the original texts of the Bible were inspired, but I'm not so sure about the translators and the interpretations that flowed from translations. Thus, while I feel comfortable and comforted by my beliefs, there is still a lot for me to explore in that realm.

Another friend, Brian Kelly, sent me an article from his college alumni magazine that also occupied my thoughts that evening. The article was written by students who had volunteered in Missionaries of Charity facilities in Kolkata. They described a one-eyed child who'd been picked up on the streets where she'd been abandoned. She was so wild that she had to be tied to the table during meals so that the sisters and volunteers could attend to other children too. She sounded to me like the gypsy children who used to populate the streets of Zagreb in the early seventies, mutilated by their parents in hopes their begging would bring in more money.

I was dismayed by one student's description of a woman at *Kalighat*— the House for Sick and Dying Destitutes—who was screaming in pain while a nurse cleaned her wounds. I'm a dogged proponent of pain management, and I'd heard that strong analgesics weren't available at Mother Teresa's facilities. To me, there's nothing harder than hurting a patient when you're trying to help. Some medical people seem to be able to numb their senses, but it takes a toll on me. I've never gotten the hang of "professional detachment."

But to put my concern in context, Indian hospitals often refuse to admit seriously ill and dying patients, so Mother Teresa's is sometimes the only medical care they can get. In addition, many "private doctors" in India are charlatans who practice without a license and can do more harm than good. For example, the executive director of the Indian aid organization Environmental Health Project (EHP) said that in the Delhi slum of

Indore, "Seventy-one percent of the slum dwellers…go to private doctors, many of whom are not licensed, and all of whom are expensive."[1]

That's shocking, but before we start feeling too high and mighty about the caliber of medical care in the United States, here's a little reality jolt: multiple studies show that the United States is seriously lacking in the areas of pain control and end-of-life care. A January 2004 study that was published in the *Journal of the American Medical Association* describes how the families of 1,578 dying patients perceived their loved ones were treated. The study concludes that most did not receive adequate treatment to ease pain and other symptoms, such as difficulty in breathing. Patients and families cited deficiencies: they did not feel they had been treated with respect, nor that they had received the emotional support they'd expected. They also felt their physicians had lacked communication skills.[2] This study is just one among many from the past few decades that have come to similar conclusions. As a hospice nurse, this problem weighed heavily on my mind long before I thought of setting foot in India. Even my own experience with pain management has been negative. In fact, the last time I had surgery, I was screaming in the recovery room before a nurse was able to persuade the doctor that I was not getting adequate pain control.

So what did I hope to achieve in India that I couldn't at home? Mother Teresa said, "You can find Calcutta all over the world, if you have eyes to see." She thought the pain of loneliness and rejection to be greater than physical hunger, and set about to heal it with human kindness. Of the distance we in the West maintain from the sick, dying, and unwanted, she said:

> I found the poverty of the West so much more difficult to remove. When I pick up a person from the street, hungry, I give him a plate of rice, a piece of bread, I have satisfied. I have removed that hunger. But a person that is shut out, that feels unwanted, unloved, terrified, the person that has been thrown out from society—that poverty is so hurtable and so much, and I find that very difficult.[3]

I agree, but I'd volunteered in America since I was thirteen years old, and I wanted to explore the philosophy of this woman who cared so much for those who had no one else. How better than to walk in her footsteps and live among those she chose to love?

WELCOME TO KOLKATA

As my Singapore Air flight began its descent, a male voice announced: "We are expecting to arrive on schedule," the first syllable pronounced "shed" as the English do. "We will be having a deplaning shortly thereafter."

Meanwhile, flight attendants sprayed the compartment with an unidentified substance that was required by Indian government regulations. They told us it was not toxic, but the whole cabin was coughing.

The ground below glittered with a million lights, but in the dark and from that height, it could have been any big city. As we neared the ground, streets came into focus, and the first thing I noticed was that they teemed with people.

It was almost eleven o'clock at night when we landed in Kolkata, the capital of the Indian state of West Bengal. The weather report was eighty-two degrees Fahrenheit and cloudy, and my face was itching from that stuff they sprayed around the cabin. I needed a bath and a costume change. I hadn't slept well for days, and to top off my discomfort, as we taxied to the gate, I caught a snippet of conversation behind me. A woman said, "Oh yes, snakes can come up the toilet during monsoons"—an unfortunate image to have in my head that first night.

While waiting to clear Customs I realized that the probing male stares I'd been warned about had begun, and I didn't like it. It made me feel like prey. In preparation for this trip, I'd gone so far as to have my hairdresser remove the red casts from my hair, because the Mother Teresa volunteers in D.C. who had spent time in Kolkata told me such a striking color would attract unwanted attention from the men who line the streets in Kolkata's poorer sections. If the leers at the airport were any gauge, the streets would be downright scary.

One Bengali woman in Washington had recommended I carry an open safety pin to jab men who groped me in crowded situations. But as I dragged my luggage through the airport, my hands were full and I wasn't up to stabbing anyone my first night in a strange country. I lowered my head and charged forward. I assumed this off-putting stance to say "don't touch" without opening my mouth. As an FBI agent who had worked the streets of Washington, D.C., and San Francisco, I had learned to use demeanor to influence others' behavior. This is the law enforcement officer's first line of defense. Fistfights and guns are a last resort.

The first glitch came as soon as I cleared Indian Customs. The driver, who was supposed to be included in my hotel room fee, was not there to meet me. This was a big problem, because Kolkata cabbies can be scoundrels.

I went back to the arrivals area and exchanged some money to call the hotel. On the first try I got a recording that said the call could not be completed as dialed. After two more tries, I resigned myself to finding a cab. A feeling of desperation swept over me as I remembered what I'd read on the plane: U.S. Department of State travelers' advisories. Here's a passage that seemed particularly poignant at that moment:

> Taxi drivers and others may solicit travelers with "come-on" offers of cheap transportation and/or hotels. Travelers accepting such offers have often found themselves the victims of scams, including disproportionately expensive hotel rooms, unwanted "tours," unwelcome "purchases," and even threats when the tourists try to decline to pay. Travelers should exercise significant care when hiring transportation and/or guides. Individual tourists have also been given drugged drinks or tainted food to make them more vulnerable to theft, particularly at train stations. Even food or drink purchased in front of the traveler from a canteen or vender could be tainted.

Some Westerners, including U.S. citizens, have been the victims of robberies, rapes, or other violent attacks. The common thread for most attacks has been that the victims were alone. U.S. citizens are cautioned not to travel alone in India.[4]

Being duly advised, I searched out a kiosk that said "prepaid taxi." Sister Nirmala had told me in her letter that prepaid was the safest way to go, and the prepaid cabs at the airport were monitored by the government. The clerk said the ticket would cost one hundred seventy nine rupees, a little more than four dollars, but when I handed him the money, he asked for ten more.

Thinking I'd misunderstood the original price, I gave him the ten rupees and waited for the receipt. He slipped the ten under the desk, put the rest in the cash drawer, and then handed me a receipt for one hundred seventy nine rupees. I was not prepared to address the issue of honesty with him at that point, so I thanked him and headed out the door.

Outside, the air was tropical, wafting the smells that humidity brings. The breeze was musty, and moisture hung thick around me. It felt nice to my Texas-born skin. I had only gone a few yards when the cabbies accosted me—masses of them. I didn't like the feel of the bum's rush I was getting, so I charged ahead repeating, "Prepaid, prepaid," and they melted away. One of them finally pointed to a yellow and black cab parked across the driveway and said, "There is prepaid."

A grinning man, slight and about 5'7" tall, threw my bag into the trunk of his aging Ambassador cab and secured the trunk with a padlocked chain. He then held the door as I climbed in. The first thing I noticed when I was settled in the back seat of the hump-backed vehicle was the wand of burning incense sticking out of the dashboard. I'd been warned about a lot of things, but I never expected an open flame in a car.

The cabby's smile and relaxed demeanor made me feel safe, though his accent was thick, and I didn't fully understand what he said. He nodded when I said Oberoi Grand, then started the cab on the third turn of the key, and we were off like a shot, gears grinding as he shifted through them. We bolted from the airport into a melee of traffic. I'd never seen so many cars in my life, and the right-of-way was on the left, so vehicles came at us in a different way than in the United States. However, from what was going on around me, I wondered whether Indian motorists could just pick whichever side they wanted to drive on. Indeed, it seemed that if a driver spotted the smallest opening, he could call kings-x without warning and dive in front of other vehicles.

I tried to remember which part of the back seat J. Edgar Hoover wouldn't sit in because he insisted it was "the death seat." Of course, there were no seat belts in the cab, so they were probably all death seats. Still, I'd heard that if you're in a wreck in Kolkata, you should slam money onto the seat and run, because angry crowds have been known to gather and attack whoever is in the vehicle. To look on the bright side, I decided to view the seat belt as an impediment in an escape and just be glad I didn't have one.

As the street vomited torrents of cabs, busses, rickshaws, and three-wheeled autos and trucks, the cabby zoomed directly into oncoming traffic. Move over, New York and Los Angeles. There's a new traffic champ in town.

If there were traffic control lights, I didn't see them, or everyone was going through them so quickly that it didn't matter. Other cabs tried to nudge their way in, but my driver was oblivious to their aggression and won every contest, much to my chagrin. At one point, he looked at me in the rearview mirror and sighed, "Kolkata. So many cars."

"I don't think the streets were built with cars in mind," came my meek reply. "There are roads in Washington, D.C. that were built for horse carts." This was the extent of our conversation.

Dwellings whizzed past—gray concrete blocks piled atop one another. At first I mistook the structures for abandoned, but now and then I could see movement, even on the upper floors. I guessed the structures were the *bustees* I'd read about, where thousands of families pile into spartan enclosures without electricity and sometimes without water or sanitation.

Although communist Eastern Europe was infinitely wealthier-looking, some aspects of these buildings reminded me of Belgrade, especially the prefabricated concrete-block style of architecture and the dirty grayness that enveloped their exteriors. Plus, it was election time, and hammers and sickles adorned virtually every wall along the way. India is the world's largest democracy, but the communist party is strong among the masses of Kolkata. Here, as in the communist countries I'd seen, indignant rhetoric bewailed the plight of the people, while a fabulously rich and powerful upper crust lived in protected seclusion.

Interspersed were ornate buildings that retained an intriguing ruined grandeur, but the streets made me feel claustrophobic—I guess because the buildings were tall and continuous. There seemed to be no break in them—no grass, trees, or parks. People crowded the sidewalks, walking, sitting, lying. Vendors squatted with their wares spread out before them: cloths, fruit, metallic plates, and utensils. A montage of scents impregnated the breeze—cinnamon, mold, and here and there, marijuana.

We passed a hospital made of concrete with wall-sized, wooden-shuttered windows gaping open. The sign said "Cardiological Emergency Hospital." Though I could see into the rooms, there was no equipment visible. I did a nursing internship in the Johns Hopkins Cardiac Surgical Intensive Care Unit, so I expected to at least see the glow of cardiac vital sign monitors in the pitch-dark rooms.

Drivers honked incessantly, and traffic moved at a break-neck speed. No one yielded, unless they got backed down by another driver who was willing to risk more. People sauntered out in front of cars and the cars didn't stop.

Yet on the sidewalks, life seemed casual. I spotted a man bathing on the curb, splashing his body with the caramel-colored water that poured from a communal pump. He was nude except for some sort of g-string that covered his genitals. Farther down stood another pump, where a woman, wearing a sari without the blouse, drenched her waist-long braid in the flowing filth. I was surprised to see her breasts partially exposed. Maybe shocked is a better word, since I was practically ready to wear a *burqa* to ensure I would not be molested.

Amid the people were many dogs, small in stature with pointy ears, like the jackals painted on the walls of Egyptian tombs, but with wiry, shepherd-like coats and curlicue tails. We zoomed by a dog lying in the middle of a side street, suckling two pups. I was amazed that she felt comfortable with her family in the midst of all those vehicles.

As we continued on our path, the streets became a little wider, and fewer people crowded the sidewalk. Suddenly, the cabby pointed up a road and said Mother Teresa's convent—also known as the Mother House, where Mother Teresa lies entombed, was about half a kilometer away at 54A Acharya Jagdish Chandra Bose Road. It looked better in the direction he was pointing than where we are.

The Oberoi Grand was two kilometers from this intersection. He added that the Circular Hotel was near the Mother House and was also nice. I'd heard the same from other Missionaries of Charity volunteers in

Washington, D.C., and I wanted to consider the Circular when deciding where to make reservations for the bulk of the trip. Another place had been recommended to me as well: Monica House, an un-air-conditioned, dormitory-style boarding house on the grounds of Saint James Episcopal Church. It was reputed to be cheap and safe, and I heard that if I was to get a real taste of Mother Teresa's India, Monica House might be the best choice.

Soon we pulled up to the horseshoe drive of the Oberoi Grand, and the doorman approached the cab wearing a pristine white uniform with a gold, braided shoulder cord. As I tipped the cabby, a bellhop loaded my luggage on a dolly. He, too, wore a white uniform and gloves. On his head was a pillbox hat with a chinstrap similar to one I remembered from a 1950s Philip Morris cigarette commercial. I relaxed, knowing that he was not going to steal my bags.

Inside the Oberoi Grand, I found an oasis amidst the turmoil of Kolkata's pulsating streets. Gone were the noises, smells, and crush of humanity. In their place was pure opulence—sweeping staircases of carved wood, along with massive chandeliers and marble floors. In my room I was greeted with fruit, bottled water, a damask-covered featherbed, and a shelf full of toiletries. My first impulse was to settle into a hot, flower-scented bubble bath, but I decided against it. I'd already gotten my first mosquito bite, and the local mosquitoes carried dengue fever and malaria—I didn't want to smell too tasty.

Despite the onslaught of this town—this Indian version of the Wild West—I already felt I was settling in. It occurred to me that I had been over-prepared for a level of poverty like nothing else on earth. What I found was not as unique as I'd imagined. Though not in these numbers, a similar desperation marks the Caribbean, where corrugated metal huts line the hills outside posh resorts. Still, I realized that what I had seen in that harried cab ride was no more than a snapshot, and a late-night one at that. I resolved that in the morning I would walk to the market and the Indian Museum and take a closer look at life on the streets. The desk clerk had said that the museum was only half a kilometer away, and the market was just out the side door. With my sense of direction, which is profoundly impaired, walking anywhere would be interesting.

CHANGE IN PLANS

What would have been a pleasant visit to the Indian Museum ended badly when I took an unexpected cab ride. Or shall I say the cab took me?

I walked to the Indian Museum, but when I started back to the hotel, I wasn't sure which way to go. This happens to me all the time, and it doesn't usually throw me——I just see more of the countryside than the average traveler. Years of getting lost have shown me the futility of worrying about it, so I go with the flow and meander around, even in unfamiliar countries.

Though disoriented and recognizing no landmarks, I was not concerned as I approached a main street crowded with sidewalk vendors. The time was about one o'clock—still plenty of daylight hours left. And the hundreds of people who crowded the avenues could give directions, if I should need them. At least, that's what I told myself as I strolled along.

My sunny outlook diminished the farther down the street I ventured. The sidewalks were wall-to-wall people, and my Western desire for arm's-length body space was battered and bruised. In that crowd, standing an inch from others seemed to be half an inch too far away for everyone but me.

Men kept trying to entice me into their stores. When I bypassed them, they pursued me down the sidewalk, asking in pleading tones why I wouldn't come in and look around. They blocked my way and accused me of not trusting them. Now and then my American politeness caused me to meet their eyes and assure them that I wasn't judging them. That was a big mistake. Once they heard me reply, they piled on the sales pitches, and I couldn't get them to back off. If I got rid of one, others appeared to take his place. I felt trapped and intimidated by this merchant hydra, and then I spotted a brand new cab parked near the curb. It was by far the nicest automobile I'd seen on the streets. Its seats were covered in plastic and there were no open flames on the dash, so I jumped in just to escape. Alas, the driver proceeded to drag me all over Kolkata and beyond.

He seemed to understand only a few words of English. He was young—no more than late twenties—with angry eyes, a leering glare, and thick unkempt facial hair. Throughout the ride he played Islamic music, which wouldn't be a problem for me, were it not for the press the United States was getting from the war in Iraq at the time.

As we barreled through town, I alternately concentrated on trying to figure out where we were and planning what to do about my predicament. Here and there, buildings looked prosperous, but none of the neighborhoods seemed inviting. And, although I didn't know much about the city layout, I quickly realized the density of buildings and people was diminishing. We crossed a bridge and my fears mounted. There was no question we were leaving Kolkata, and I didn't know where we were headed or what I was going to do about it.

My mind was abuzz with gloomy thoughts. The worst-case scenario was that he would take me hostage. How ironic that the woman who supervised the FBI's response to international hijackings in the mid-1980s could end up a hostage herself. Plus, my son was deployed "somewhere in the War on Terrorism," and now Mommy's a hostage herself. How's that for irony?

As I pondered a life of captivity, I tried to envision a map. The Howrah Bridge leads across the Hugli River into Howrah, but the Howrah Bridge is a steel structure, and I had no recollection of anything but concrete whizzing by. At that point though, I was concentrating more on prayer than construction materials.

To make it all the more surreal, the scenes that whizzed by became increasingly peaceful. The housing looked impoverished but, because there were fewer people per square kilometer, it didn't seem as desperate as in the downtown area. A velvety tan bovine stood halfway in the doorway of an open hovel, where a woman was hanging clothes from a line that stretched from the house to a tree. A stream ran by the structure and people were casually washing themselves in it. It was serene and bucolic, yet it did nothing to relieve the knots in my shoulders.

We passed the Sheraton, a tall, modern building rising from a sandy, almost desert-like terrain. As glad as I was to glimpse a talisman of the West while being swept along to heaven knows what, the juxtaposition of the Sheraton was jarring. I wondered what hotel guests thought as they stared out from their Western accommodations. At least in my hotel, the most luxurious of all, the windows faced an internal courtyard where I didn't see the world around me and could live comfortably in denial.

Several times I pleaded, "This is not the way;" and each time the driver responded in an angry tone, "Yes, yes, Oberoi Grand."

As he spoke through gritted teeth, he turned his head enough for me to see an unusual amount of wideness to his eyes. They were the eyes of druggies in the midst of mania, the kind who don't feel pain when bullets tear their skin and keep on charging at you until they bleed to death.

It was ever-present on my mind that some Kolkata men consider Western women to be loose, immodest, and not deserving of respect. This impression was bolstered by the pictures of American movie stars plastered across Kolkata newspapers, their necklines plunging to their navels. My blouse and jumper dress covered me from neck to ankles, but I was not veiled and this man was obviously a Muslim.

The temperature outside was in the mid-nineties, even more in the un-air-conditioned cab—especially with my blood pressure spiking as I agonized over whether I should jump from the cab into a possibly worse unknown or stick with the devil I was getting to know. My complete disorientation as we raced down crowded alleys made me opt to stay in the cab. I doubt that many on the street would be interested in my plight. They certainly had other things to worry about.

At last we made a U-turn at a cul-de-sac and headed back toward town. When we arrived at the Oberoi, the cabby wanted one hundred eighty rupees, a usurious price for what should have been a few minutes' ride. One hundred eighty rupees was a little over four dollars, but the man had kept me in the car for over an hour and scared the begeebers out of me, so I reported him to the hotel doorman. The doorman promised to call the police and ban the driver from the hotel to prevent him from victimizing other guests.

I returned to my room to rest and write in my journal, but I couldn't unwind after that interlude of unadulterated fear. Also, my jaw ached from clenching my teeth during the ride. I felt like a fool for putting myself in this position and wondered how far from the hotel I'd been when I jumped into that cab. Unable to let go of the tension that had mounted during the ride, I ventured outside for a few minutes and realized that, from the edge of the Oberoi's driveway, I could see the spot where I'd hailed the cab. If I had not panicked, it would have taken me no more than two or three minutes to walk back.

This cab ride made it painfully clear how naïve I could be at times. My motto has been to treat people well and they will reciprocate, and in the depths of my heart, I still believe it. Nevertheless, you'd think that thirteen years of chasing fugitives, extortionists, and terrorists as an FBI agent would have taught me to be more suspicious. In a way, I think succeeding in law enforcement worked against me. I had survived situations that most women never encounter, and I'd gained confidence that was possibly misplaced. I had no illusions that I could easily out-wrestle or disarm a big man, and I understood the obvious things, such as that I should be wary when walking into crowds or down secluded back streets in dangerous places. Nevertheless, person by person, I still tended to trust. It is both my best and worst trait, and it frustrates me when my trust leads me to place myself in jeopardy.

Furious with myself, I couldn't relax, so I settled by the pool to read the newspapers and divert my thoughts. I hoped the news would help me gain an understanding of this whirlwind I had dived into.

The Hindustan Times reported that Rabindranath Tagore's Nobel medallion and some other memorabilia had been stolen in March. It was the latest in a string of thefts from the Tagore collection.[5]

Tagore (1861-1941) was a Bengali who won the Nobel Prize for his poetry in 1913 "because of his profoundly sensitive, fresh and beautiful verse, by which, with consummate skill, he has made his poetic thought, expressed in his own English words, a part of the literature of the West."[6]

Tagore is revered for his poetry, essays, stories, music, art, and drama. He was a friend of Gandhi's who lived his life under the rule of the British Empire. Here's an excerpt from his work, *Gitanjali*.

Where the mind is without fear and the head is held high;
Where knowledge is free;
Where the world has not been broken up into fragments

By narrow domestic walls;
Where words come out from the depth of truth;
Where tireless striving stretches its arms towards perfection;
Where the clear stream of reason has not lost its way
Into the dreary desert sand of dead habit;
Where the mind is led forward by thee
Into ever-widening thought and action—
Into that heaven of freedom, my Father, let my country awake.[7]

What would Tagore say of the Kolkata I experienced today, the seamier side, where women live in fear? There has been progress. Bengal, along with the rest of India, freed herself from the bonds of the British Empire, but cruelty and difficult lives remain without the oppression of a foreign yoke.

As for me, I sat safe and cool in a lounge chair by the Oberoi's pool and my fears subsided. I considered how lucky I was not to have become a hostage and vowed not to put myself in the position to be victimized again.

The air around me was humid, but the caressing breeze made it pleasantly cool as I lolled in the poolside gardens. The vegetation reminded me of the Caribbean, except for the huge palms, which were taller than the five-story hotel and seemed more spectacular than those of the islands. Scattered among greenery was a profusion of flowering vines and plants: orange day lilies, pink and gold zinnias, white peace lilies, pink oleanders, lush green ferns, red bougainvilleas, fuchsia ravenias, pink periwinkles, huge gold sunflowers with their chocolate centers, and a deep green bushy plant with yellow conical blooms made up of school-bus yellow waxy leaf-like petals interspersed with white petals of the same texture.

Sprinkled throughout the garden were huge black birds, pigeons, and the ubiquitous brown bird. I remembered how shocked I'd been to see the little brown ones in the East Berlin train station years ago, just after the Wall had fallen. Knowing nothing about ornithology, I'd always assumed these birds were native to the United States. I have to say, in India, I expected more color—like in a tropical rain forest.

The guttering around the pool, combined with an exotic, gently bubbling aeration system, caused it to overflow its bounds like a cup of water when a few extra drops drive it over the edge. It was an appealing and peaceful design that kept the surface flat yet flowing. When someone jumped in, its glass-like surface churned to a rolling boil and made a sound as if a giant plug had been pulled and was sucking the water into a vortex—an appropriate metaphor for today's cab ride.

In consideration of this day's events, I decided to stay an extra night at the Oberoi Grand, forgo Monica House, and arrange for the more Western accommodations that the Circular Hotel had to offer. Government-approved, the Circular offered air-conditioned single rooms for seven hundred thirty rupees per night, which was less than twenty dollars at the time. It had its own restaurant, which looked quite nice, and was located across from the Mother House, so I couldn't get lost on the way to mass in the mornings.

As I prepared for moving closer to the Missionaries of Charity, another Tagore quote came to mind. In his lecture, *Crisis in Civilisation*, he spoke of the British Empire. In some ways, it could describe Mother Teresa's Kolkata:

> As I look around I see the crumbling ruins of a proud civilisation strewn like a vast heap of futility. And yet I shall not commit the grievous sin of losing faith in Man. I would rather look forward to the opening of a new chapter in his history after the cataclysm is over and the atmosphere rendered clean with the spirit of service and sacrifice.[8]

Reading this man's philosophy, one can see how Mother Teresa grew to love the Bengalis, not just as her life's mission of service, but as a culture whose people and traditions she would aid but not seek to change. In the month that would follow, I would fight her will to help without imposing other countries' values and her desire that volunteers learn to live as Indians, rather than that Indians live as we do in the West.

KALIGHAT AT LAST

Before my first day at *Kalighat*, I went to six o'clock mass at the Mother House. Then, after breakfast, I took a bus to the House for Sick and Dying Destitutes. Officially named *Nirmal Hriday*, meaning "the pure heart," it was Mother Teresa's first home for her beloved poor. Because it's adjacent to the Kali Temple, *Nirmal Hriday* is now called—even by the Missionaries of Charity—*Kalighat*.

A woman I met at breakfast, Phillis Wong Hwee Ne, a tall and lovely pharmaceutical engineer from Singapore, helped me navigate the bus system from the Mother House to *Kalighat*. Her easy laugh and soft voice were welcoming. Although she appeared to be in her twenties, she was a seasoned world traveler and confident in finding her way around Kolkata.

The bus dropped us off a couple of blocks from *Kalighat* near the Hawkers' Corner market area, and we walked down the long corridor of street vendors that dot the aisles leading to the Kali Temple. *Ghat*—the second half of *Kalighat*—means "a river landing." Before sediment accumulated in the delta, Kali Temple was situated on a tributary of the Hugli River, which is itself a tributary of the Ganges. The tributary dried up, but during colonial days a canal was dug, restoring the area's *ghat*. *Ghat* can also mean "steps," ala "in Kali's steps."

Known as the "Black One," Kali is the fearsome and fearsomely protective mother goddess from whom the city draws its name. Her depictions personify death and destruction, with a blood-crimson tongue protruding from her mouth and a third eye in the center of her forehead. Nevertheless, Bengalis see her as a protective goddess who saved the world by killing thousands of demons. Her tongue is red because she lapped up the demons' blood before it could hit the ground where it would spawn more demons, and that is why Bengalis believe Kali is powerful enough to kill death and protect those she loves.

The Kali Temple was built in 1809 on the site of an ancient temple. It remains a place of worship and a place where the dying come for their final blessing. The building that adjoined the temple had been a *dormashalah* (pilgrims' hostel) before it became Mother Teresa's *Nirmal Hriday*.

In contrast to the ornate and colorful Kali Temple, which is also famous for its art, Mother's House for Sick and Dying Destitutes is spartan on the inside. Its ground floor is split into two sides—men's and women's—and every surface of the structure is stone or tiled so it can be hosed down and scrubbed. The floor of each wing is in two heights, each of which accommodates a row of cots. On the lower level is one row, and a meter-high stair-step landing holds an additional tier. On the cots are bright blue mattresses with green sheets of a loose cotton weave. Volunteers and sisters move up and down the aisles as they care for their charges, and most of the time, at least fifty beds per side are full. The high-ceilinged rooms are cooled by ceiling fans and lit mainly by sun that streams through large, arched windows.

In the back of the patient wards are showers, and there is a small open area near the entrance where medications are kept and new admissions evaluated. Also, there is a walled-off area between the men's and women's sides that is used for dish—and clothes-washing.

Extra medical supplies, such as bandages, are kept in an attic that leads off from the washing area and can only be accessed by climbing a steep concrete staircase. The stairs are so narrow that I hugged the wall as I ascended. I felt as if one slip of the foot would make me plummet over the side to the concrete floors below. The attic itself was no safer. It was dimly lit and the window-less loft, which was crowded with boxes, had no guardrails.

On the story above the patient ward were a surprisingly small kitchen with propane burners, a sewing area, and a little veranda where the volunteers took tea breaks. There was also a chapel and an open-air dining area where the sisters ate—or so I assumed, as volunteers never saw the sisters eat. Beyond that area were some rooms I never entered.

The standing instructions for volunteers were to attend prayers at the beginning of each shift, help pass out food, then start working wherever they wanted. Tasks included bathing and massaging patients, washing dishes and cloth items, cleaning the facility, assisting in medical procedures, passing out medications, sitting with patients, and attending to the myriad unexpected tasks that came up in a day.

The Missionaries of Charity emphasize holistic healing, which, like hospice, concentrates on the whole patient—mind, body, and soul—and combines the miracle pills of the modern medical science with Eastern therapies, such as massage, a time-proven pain and anxiety reliever. An added benefit is that the oil helps keep the skin healthy.

I was also relieved to learn that English was the official language of the Missionaries of Charity order, so at least I could communicate with all of the sisters and they could translate when I needed to speak with patients. I told one of the long-term volunteers that I was a nurse and asked where I could help. She responded that the kitchen needed dish-dryers, so I should grab a towel after prayers. As I glanced toward the kitchen, Carolyn Milton, a pert, twenty-five-year-old Australian emergency department nurse, said with in a tone of exasperation, "That's not a nursing duty, and there are too many bandages for me to take care of alone. Why don't you come with me?"

I told her that wounds and pain control were my specialties, and she replied, "Thank goodness. I've been the only nurse for a while because our mainstay, Susan, is in hospital. I'll help you get your bandage tray together after prayers, then you can take half the women and I'll take the other." With that, we joined the sisters and the rest of the volunteers for prayers in the small open area between the men's and women's wards.

Each Missionaries of Charity prayer service includes the "Collaborators with Mother Teresa daily prayer":

Love make me a channel of your peace,
That where there is hatred
I may bring love;
Where there is injustice,
I may bring the spirits of forgiveness;
Where there is discord,
I may bring harmony;

Where there is error,
I may bring truth;
Where there is doubt,
I may bring faith;
Where there is despair,
I may bring hope;
Where there is shadows,
I may bring light;
Where there is sadness,
I may bring love;
Lord, grant that I may seek rather to comfort
Than to be comforted;
To understand than to be understood;
To love than to be loved;
For it is by forgetting that one finds himself;
It is by forgiving that one is forgiven;
It's by dying that one awakens to eternal life.

After that respite, chaos ensued. Those bandaging grappled for available supplies. Novices and nurses caring for the women's side had be quick because the Missionaries of Charity brothers came through like a raiding party, grabbing bandage supplies for the men's side. While the novices showed deference to them, we nurses scrapped for what the women needed. I'm sure it was culturally improper for two Western nurses to nudge out these men at the supply cabinet, but we did. Back in the States, most nurses from small hospices and hospitals keep a secret stash for when supplies run low. Used to the "by hook or crook" method of stocking, I felt at home.

I soon learned that premium items at *Kalighat* were gloves and hydro-colloid dressing pads—a special type of wound covering that promotes a moist wound bed and is only changed every three to five days. One reason these heal long-term wounds so well is they can't stick to the wound bed, so they don't pull off healing tissue when they are changed. Also, though they are not airtight, they keep the wound cleaner than gauze. Instinctively, I concealed a couple of extras in my apron for deep, chronic wounds.

Not seeing the wound-cleansing products I'd hoped for, I consulted Dr. Fong, a twinkling-eyed doctor from Singapore who was volunteering a couple of weeks of his time. With him was his eighteen-year-old daughter, Margaret. Dr. Fong explained a few alternatives among available supplies—hydrogen peroxide and an iodine solution that could be further weakened with normal saline solution—and I was ready to get started. Carolyn took one end of the women's ward, and I took the other. For the rest of the time, we were so busy that we could hardly wave at each other.

Mother's facilities are missionary homes that open their doors to people in need. They are not hospitals, but the type of care administered mirrors the host country's medical traditions. In Baltimore, for example, they follow the city's health codes and send their patients to Johns Hopkins when they require medical care. In their home, they administer the medications as prescribed by the doctors, just like a family would.

In India, there are traditional medical practices as well as contemporary Western. As much as I believe in Western ways of healing, I know that traditional Indian and Chinese medical practices are used to treat more than half of the world's population. In China, massage, herbs, Tai Chi, and meditation for stress reduction are commonly prescribed regimes. They also conduct major surgery using acupuncture as anesthesia.

In India, there is the ancient system of natural healing known as *Ayurveda*, a word derived from the Sanskrit *ayur* (life) and *veda* (knowledge). *Ayurvedic* practice treats the mind, body, and soul to keep them in tune with the five elements of nature: space *(akash)*, air *(vayu)*, fire *(agni)*, water *(jala)*, and earth *(prithvi)*.

Very simply put, *Ayurvedics* concentrate on three biological forces: *vata*, *pitta*, and *kapha*. *Vata*, which is based upon air and space, controls flow and motion, including physical locomotion and the respiratory and circulatory systems. It also concerns thought, creativity, and fear. The fire and water elements are addressed through *pitta*, which governs functions associated with heat and metabolism, as well as emotions such as anger and pride. Finally, *kapha* represents water and earth. It concentrates on the structure and coordination of physiology, also love and negative emotions, such as greed and jealousy.

Ayurvedic interventions for disease include yoga, massage, meditation, and herbs. So well respected are Ayurveda and the Islamic practice of Unani that they are official parts of the Indian national health program by law and many providers are graduates of university degree programs.

Even the U.S. medical establishment is coming around on complementary therapies, and many U.S. medical research centers are beginning to incorporate Eastern medical principles into practice. I, on the other hand, know little about these centuries-old arts, so my default thinking is Western.

Kalighat had no permanent medical staff, not even an on-call doctor, though an Indian doctor came by a few hours a week, and sometimes other doctors volunteered. Professionally trained nursing staff consisted of one Chinese sister and the volunteers. While this concept sounds wholly inadequate to American ears, in this tough West Bengal city where the government decrees free medical care, hospitals refuse to treat seriously ill and dying patients when they choose, especially those without money. This dirty little secret was, in fact, rather well known to the people of Kolkata. While I was there, *The Times of India* reported that the Friends Foundation of Asia would open Kolkata's first true hospice. The article reads:

> Have you been refused a bed at the nursing home because you are terminally ill, or suffering from a contagious disease?...Well, a new facility, which will become operational from next month, can provide that ray of hope for all such distressed patients in the city. For the first time in Kolkata, a voluntary organization, called Friends Foundation of Asia, is starting a hospice at Narendrapur for the benefit of all those patients who are denied admission in hospitals or nursing homes.[9]

But this hospice had not yet opened, and Mother Teresa's volunteers and sisters were the only alternative to the government's "free" medical aid. For decades the sisters have attempted to fill the void with care and respect for anyone who crosses their threshold. For some of their charges, being regarded as a human being is a new experience.

The ramifications of providing healthcare in a place run by missionaries instead of doctors and nurses were difficult to get through my nursing head. I had to adjust to not having access to the information I had come to expect in American hospitals. At *Kalighat*, there were no charts with diagnoses or medical histories, only lists of medications ordered, with injections in one book and pills in the other. Both were written in pencil because the nurses changed the orders as needed.

Since I was bandaging, I didn't give out medications that first morning, so I had yet to learn that choosing medications was a nursing task. In

India, most drugs are sold without prescription. Anyone can walk up to a chemist shop and buy antibiotics, for example, so it was fine for nurses to choose medications for the patients. In fact, the chemists I encountered were store clerks, not pharmacists, as I found out when they handed me the wrong medication a couple of times. After I realized that, I always printed the medication and dose I wanted in big block letters so they could compare the label on the box to the paper.

As crazy as all this may sound to nurses in the United States, the system works. Indeed, the value of *Kalighat* cannot be measured against the American way of medicine. *Kalighat* is an expression of the Missionaries of Charity's love, and patients are healed because they are given tender care, an important quality that is scarce in the high-tech whirl of contemporary American medicine. That is not to say that the pace of the nursing floor at *Kalighat* was sluggish. To the contrary, there were so many patients that the nurses rarely had a chance to consult or help each other. We had to be very independent and resourceful. I liked that, but then I had no idea the extent to which the next few weeks would test my nursing ingenuity.

INTO THE WHIRLWIND

Sitting on the cot and watching my every move as if she were a student, was a tall, smiling woman with shaven, graying stubble on her head. Her name was Lavanya, and her head had been shaved because she had had lice when she came in from the streets. Examining her, I discovered multiple wounds on her legs and buttocks. I was told these wounds had been infected and life threatening when she came in. They looked like decubitus ulcers—also known as pressure or bedsores—but I wasn't concerned about the exact origin just then. It didn't matter, because the wounds were clean and well cared for, so I knew what to do with them.

On her shins, the wounds were so deep that I could see the muscles retract when she moved. As bad as that sounds, the plan of care is fairly simple from a nursing perspective:

1.   Keep the wound bed clean and moist.
2.   Keep the skin around the wound bed dry.
3.   Make sure the patient does not apply unnecessary pressure to damaged areas.
4.   Instruct the patient to eat a healthy diet.

Wounds like these occur when people are very ill and can't eat, if they have nerve damage and can't feel, or if they can't shift their weight. These ulcers are the bane of every hospice and long-term care facility in the world, even the best of them. It is vital that such deep wounds stay moist to heal, but a quick look at the patients who filled all the beds in the women's ward told me that the few hydrocolloid dressings I'd concealed in my apron for such situations were not nearly enough for the number of wounds that lay ahead of me that morning.

I decided to save the precious hydrocolloid dressings for spinal wounds, because the hydrocolloids are gel-like and less bulky to lie on than gauze dressings. This meant I'd have to use gauze on Lavanya's shins, so I'd grabbed a jar of viscous wound cream from Hong Kong and piled it onto the gauze to keep it moist and prevent it from sticking to the wound until tomorrow's bandage change.

After I'd dressed her wounds, Lavanya suddenly spoke. In proper British English, she asked, "Will I return to home within one month?"

There was a chance she could heal by then, but the course of healing varies with disease and nutrition. Not having a medical history or laboratory tests left so many unknowns in Lavanya's case, so I wasn't willing to predict a date.

"We'll work on the wounds," I said, "but you must eat well and walk as much as you can. These are the things that will help you heal." She smiled and nodded thoughtfully.

Later, Carolyn told me that Lavanya was trained as a physical therapist, but was found wandering the streets, delirious from fever and infected wounds. A wealthy woman, she held a Ph.D., but because of some family problem, she had landed on the street. No one knew the exact circumstances.

On the next cot sat Jaya, another smiling woman, pleasantly plump, with grossly swollen lower extremities and deep wounds all over her shins and feet. The pink wound beds formed a stark contrast to the deep blackness of her skin. We shared no common language, but we managed to communicate with our facial expressions and the tone of our voices. While I worked, she spoke to me as if I understood her every word, even nodding as if I'd said something interesting when I said I had no idea what she was talking about.

Because her lower extremities were puffed with fluid, known as edema in medical terminology, Jaya's condition was more challenging than Lavanya's. I examined her legs and feet, hoping to find a clue to the cause of the edema, because it would influence the care I'd plan for her. Common causes are deep venous thromboses (blood clots, also known as DVTs), arterial and venous insufficiency (poor circulation in veins or arteries), and lymphedema (an obstruction in the lymphatic system, the system that draws off fluids that escape from blood vessels and is also involved in the body's immune response to fight off infection).

Blood clots tend to cause pain and swelling near their location. Jaya's edema was widely dispersed and equal on each side, so it probably wasn't DVT. Arterial and venous insufficiencies can result in terrible wounds. This condition, however, has telltale signs, such as skin color changes or pain when the legs are in certain positions. Jaya had none of these signs. Also, it would be highly unusual for arterial or venous insufficiencies to cause such widespread edema.

Although wounds like hers are rarely caused by lymphedema alone, the look and feel of Jaya's legs indicated it was the likely cause. The skin felt thick, and the entire lower half of her legs was grossly swollen, instead of swelling on just one side or in one location. When I pressed along her bones, it did not leave an indentation, except at the feet. If the skin pits when you press in on it, as with Jaya's feet, the tissues are swollen with fluid that can be relieved—at least to an extent—by elevating the affected area. The non-pitting variety, which is much harder to relieve, is characteristic of lymphedema. In the end, I suspected lymphedema and made notes to myself to ensure she was taking a diuretic and elevating her feet as much as possible, so that gravity would shift the fluids from them.

I tended to her wounds, taking great care when I removed the tape from her dressings to pull the skin away from the tape instead of the tape away from the skin, because this method causes less trauma to the intact tissues. Healthcare workers who rip tape off can rip skin off along with it, which I'd seen done by surgeons more than anyone else.

In Jaya's case, the bandage itself had dried to the wound. I poured saline over the gauze to soak it, but I knew it would hurt when I removed it, and I'd already learned there were no strong analgesics available. I asked a passing sister to assure Jaya I'd be as gentle as possible, and Jaya responded through the translator: "You are very gentle." I worked the bandage off as humanely as I could, and when I finished, Jaya nodded with satisfaction.

As I proceeded down the line of cots, I noted that most of the women had smiles on their faces. Many were malnourished and riddled with disease. All day long I wondered: why were these women smiling?

As I continued through my hectic nursing rounds that morning, I grew increasingly sorry that I hadn't packed my own stethoscope and blood pressure cuff, because *Kalighat*'s donated equipment was of poor quality. The stethoscopes were more like the disposable equipment we had to use in ICU isolation rooms. They were cheap, but not sensitive enough to discern breath sounds on more than a crude level. I admit I'm spoiled by the quality of my stethoscope at home, but the nuances of sound are vital to determining what is going on inside a chest.

My second regret was not bringing a tropical medicine textbook. What I didn't know about tropical medicine could have filled one of those books. I didn't know, for example, what the early stages of leprosy looked like, and I'd never seen or read about most of the parasites I was to encounter during the trip.

From the first day, I longed for an international drug information handbook. Drugs and other care products at *Kalighat* were labeled in a number of different languages: Hindi, Chinese, Czech, Spanish, French, Italian, English, and German, to name a few. Some were pharmaceuticals; some were herbal. I won't use products without knowing the ingredients, so I had to dig through the hundreds of packets, bottles, and ampoules to find familiar items. I did find two drug information handbooks, but they weren't organized in a user-friendly way and took some getting used to. Fortunately, I have studied Czech, and generic drug names are sometimes similar to English in the Spanish, French, Italian, and German versions— but not always.

I soon learned that safety equipment for nurses and volunteers was also lacking, at least by U.S. standards. They had surgical masks, but not the TB masks that are approved for use in the U.S., and there were lots of tuberculosis patients. In the U.S., we believe that surgical masks work fine for most procedures, but protecting healthcare workers from TB requires a thicker mask that seals around the nose and mouth. Welcome to the Third World. Still, though I cared for many TB patients at *Kalighat* and was certainly close enough to breathe in airborne organisms, I would test negative after my return.

The oxygen tanks were so old that I was afraid they were rusted through and might blow up. Again, I'm spoiled by the slick technology of medicine in the United States, where oxygen comes out of walls instead of tanks, and you press buttons on machines to control the rate of IV drips instead of calculating the rate using a formula, then hand-adjusting the flow by counting drops while you time them with your watch. Nevertheless, the manual method works and does not depend upon electricity.

On a work-process level, a practice that drove me insane at first was not initialing the patient record at the time the medications were given to make it clear which medications had been given when. My accommodation to this was that if I gave the afternoon injections, I would be the only one giving them, so I felt assured no one would get double-dosed because two nurses who didn't speak a common language had a miscommunication. As for pills, I only gave out emergency drugs that I ordered and let the others pass out routine medications. But the fact that nurses across the world have different training and different opinions on how patients should be treated is among the reasons the sisters tell us to do only what we're comfortable with. This conflict in practice was never harder for me than in the case of Kavita.

Kavita's husband threw her into a fire and left her for dead. Days passed before neighbors brought her to *Kalighat*. When I met her, she was lying on a cot, IVs in both arms, legs bandaged to mid-thigh, and teeth grinding as she groaned. When her eyes opened, they darted furtively around, and she hugged her stomach, writhing in pain.

It was hard to guess Kavita's age. She could have been twenty or forty, and her hair was either shaven or singed short by fire. Her teeth showed ivory against the sable-colored skin, but her face had pink patches here and there where the epidermis had been burned away.

She was painfully thin—one hundred pounds at most—yet her abdomen protruded like a pregnancy. That was an ominous sign, because I was told that her abdomen had been flat the day before.

"She's in such pain," a volunteer beckoned me, asking that I examine Kavita.

An older European nurse I'll call Thomasina considered Kavita her personal charge. No one else had specific patients assigned to them, but I'd been told not to change Kavita's bandages because Thomasina was to handle all procedures for "her" patients. I glanced around for Thomasina, but she was nowhere to be found, and I concluded that she had left for the day. I didn't feel like I was stepping on toes in taking care of this patient, since I was doing what even a nursing student trained in physical assessment would have done.

I placed both hands on Kavita's belly and determined that the tip of her bladder was a finger's width beneath the umbilicus. In a normal exam, you either can't feel the bladder or it is very low in the pelvis, but I could trace the lines of Kavita's like a pregnant uterus. Her belly, however, had stretched to capacity overnight, not over nine months; and since I've had bladder colic from kidney stones, I know it hurts like hell when the bladder spasms in an attempt to expel what it cannot.

An Indian doctor, who volunteered his services, was making rounds, so I did him the courtesy of discussing my findings with him. In the United States, a urinary catheterization can usually be initiated at a nurse's discretion, but I was still feeling my way at *Kalighat*. I told the doctor I wanted to insert a Foley catheter—a urinary catheter that is used to drain the bladder. It is called in-dwelling because it stays in place when you inflate a balloon in the bladder, as opposed to a straight or in-and-out catheter, which is a one-time-use device. The doctor asked me where I'd graduated from nursing school, and I told him I'd studied in the United States. He agreed without further questions.

Unfortunately for Kavita, gathering the materials ended up taking a good half hour, because the supplies are not neatly collected in one place, and there was no such thing as a pre-packaged sterile catheterization tray like we have in the United States. While I was doing that, a nun, led by Thomasina, decided that Kavita "had too many tubes already."

"Besides," she said, "she was urinating yesterday."

With that, the sister ordered me not to catheterize Kavita.

I didn't blame the sister for not understanding, but Thomasina should have known that a bladder obstruction can occur in seconds, and what happened the day before is irrelevant when you see a suddenly swollen abdomen like Kavita's. Thomasina had been taking care of Kavita for days and knew that her abdomen was normally flat. In addition, Kavita was rubbing her distended abdomen and crying in pain. When a burn patient is crying about pain other than the burns, you better believe it's significant pain.

Relieving a rigid abdomen caused by a bladder obstruction is a medical emergency, because the bladder can rupture and peritonitis—a life-threatening infection that disperses throughout the abdomen—is likely to result. But Thomasina decided to give furosemide IV push—rapid infusion—instead of catheterizing the patient, and the doctor deferred to her opinion. I was nonplussed. Kavita's problem was not that she couldn't form urine; she couldn't pass it. Furosemide is a strong diuretic when delivered IV, and all it would do in Kavita's case was dump more fluid into her already over-filled bladder. And it wouldn't be a gentle process. Before we give furosemide IV in the ICUs, the practice is to empty a urinary collection bag—which holds at least two liters—because urine pours into the bag once the drug stimulates the renal system, and it is important to ensure there is room. An additional problem is that when you give the drug this way, you have to make sure you don't take off too much fluid and throw the body into life-threatening crisis. At *Kalighat*, we had no way of determining when Kavita had lost too much, because we didn't have access to laboratory facilities.

That's not all. Since so much of the outer layer of Kavita's skin had been burned off, she was already losing fluids through those wounds, which was obvious because the bandages were soggy. This meant that she was also leaking electrolytes such as potassium, which affects how the heart works. Adding furosemide would be a real one-two punch since it causes the body to excrete potassium, and the result of administering that drug to a burn patient without monitoring cardiac function can be fatal.

There were still other reasons to catheterize Kavita, comfort being one of them. The collection bag would keep her bandages urine-free, and she would not have to be jostled so often to be cleaned when she urinated. A catheter would also help keep the intact skin dry, so it wouldn't macerate—that is, break down from being wet—and form ulcers. From my experience as a burn tech in the Johns Hopkins Regional Burn Center ICU while I was in nursing school, I know that a burn patient's skin can form ulcers in a couple of hours.

As a nurse in the United States, I would have fought Thomasina and the doctor, no matter what the consequences. Here, the doctor acceded to her wishes, changed the order, and I backed down.

Angry and frustrated, I walked over to Carolyn's side of the floor to seek her counsel. Though she was half my age, she had more years in nursing than I. She agreed wholeheartedly with the catheterization but said I should expect to encounter medical situations at *Kalighat* wherein my American nursing training would conflict with the choices made. She said that Thomasina comes to *Kalighat* for six months out of the year, so the sisters rely upon her. Then she brushed back a wisp of her shiny brown hair and looked me in the eye. "You've got to fight for what you think is right," she said. "But you also have to be careful. People get insulted easily, and that doctor has already had some of the Western nurses removed for arguing with him."

Then and there, I vowed to find a way to resolve situations in the patients' favor. This would be a challenge if the to-the-mat patient-advocate attitude expected of nurses in the U.S. would be viewed as insulting the doctor instead of advocating for the patient. I had already sensed that he was miffed that I'd palpated an abdomen all by myself and interrupted him with what I thought was an emergency. In the United States, it would have been seen as irresponsible—or malpractice—had I not. Besides, the doctor had agreed with my conclusion when he initially looked at the patient, though I noted he did not lay a finger on her abdomen or even approach the patient.

It would be two days before Kavita was catheterized—two torturous days for her, I'm sure. I am ashamed that when I saw the nurse who prevented me from catheterizing Kavita before, "I told you so" flashed across my mind. Kavita had suffered needlessly while Thomasina defended her territory. This kind of jealousy happens every day in stateside hospitals too, but here in this atmosphere of caring and devotion to humanity, it seemed particularly out of place.

Nonetheless, I would be working with this nurse and doctor for weeks to come, and I knew they were not bad at heart. I tried to put my angry thoughts behind me and refocus. Mother Teresa said, "Words which do not give the light of Christ, increase the darkness." I knew she'd say the same thing goes for my disgruntled thoughts, and I truly wanted to follow her ways—to stretch a little spiritually and not let my ego lead me to dwell on other people's errors. No doubt, Thomasina realized what she had done and didn't need me to chastise her.

Though I can think of nothing that runs more contrary to my stubborn nature, I tried to focus on changing what I could and accepting what I could not change. Fortunately, it was easy enough to lose myself in the brisk pace of nursing and the needs of so many other critical patients. And, while I still felt I had failed Kavita, I realized it had been correct to move on, because the rest of the patients had a right to medical attention as well. The clinical term for deciding what you can treat and what you must leave to God is triage, and it is one of the most humbling tasks in medicine. All healthcare workers have a desire to help and a bit of ego in thinking we can change the course of nature. Triaging patients, as I did when I decided to leave Kavita and treat others, forced me to say the dirtiest words in the profession: "There's nothing I can do to help." Until Kolkata, I had never had to say that.

Inadequate though my nursing knowledge seemed to me at times, I noticed that people had already begun to trust me. On my way out that first morning, one of the sisters said, "I'm so glad you're here. You seemed to know just what to do." All I could think was, "Boy, did I have her fooled."

LOVING CARE

Today, I met Sister Nirmala, the current head of the Missionaries of Charity. At the time, I was changing a patient's bandage and didn't realize who she was until she began to speak with me. She was sweet and unassuming, dressed in her white cotton sari with cheap but sturdy sandals.

Still involved in my patient, I said I was pleased to meet her and went on with my work.

Sister Nirmala, who refuses to be called "mother" as would be her right, smiled and asked where I was from. Her joyous aura was hard to resist, so I told her I was from the Baltimore/Washington, D.C. area and that the sisters in Washington had asked me to convey their regards. I mentioned Sister Jonathan and Sister Regis specifically. Sister Nirmala laughed as if she'd received a wonderful gift, then she moved on and I went back to my patient.

The funny thing is that I'd had a similar experience with then-FBI director Louis Freeh. After I resigned from the FBI, I met Director Freeh at a hospice where I was a volunteer. I'd been summoned from work because my patient, an FBI assistant director, was dying. As I rushed to the patient's beside, Deputy Director Dave Binnie said, "Rosemary, I'd like you to meet someone." The dark-haired man standing next to him shoved out his hand and said, "Hi, I'm Louie Freeh."

"Nice to meet you," I said, shaking his hand. Then off I went to my patient's bed, thinking, "Louie Freeh, Louie Freeh...Where have I heard that name?"

Like Sister Nirmala, Director Freeh had smiled and had not demanded my attention. It was obvious that they both preferred I attend to patients rather than acknowledge their presence. This is a special kind of grace that is rare among those in positions of power, and so it was with Mother Teresa.

On October 7, 1950, Pope Pius XII granted permission for Mother Teresa to found the Missionaries of Charity, an order of nuns who would join her in serving the poor. On August 22, 1952, my second birthday, she established *Nirmal Hriday*, the House for Sick and Dying Destitutes. Since then she and her Missionaries of Charity have founded hundreds more in North, Central and South America, the Caribbean, Africa, Europe, the former Soviet Union, and throughout Asia. The Missionaries now consist of both sisters and brothers. Working alongside them are lay missionaries and over a million coworkers who also serve those no one else wants. Of course, the group would not be complete without the countless volunteers.

Mother Teresa sought dignity for all. No job was too dirty for her. In fact, it is said that when she visited *Kalighat*, the first thing she did was clean the toilets. The sisters who follow her take on the vows of poverty, chastity, and service to the poor while maintaining the spirit of cheerfulness that Mother Teresa exuded.

Prayer was the source of her strength. She said: "Without prayer no faith; without faith no love; without love no service; without service no joy, no peace."[10]

Mother Teresa died on September 5, 1997. By then there were Missionaries of Charity facilities worldwide. Her theory was, if you have four sisters, you can start a new facility, and thus the homes multiplied as the order's ranks swelled.

Like Mother Teresa, focus on prayer drives the Missionaries of Charity; even to the point that they pass the responsibility of patient care to volunteers and employees so that the sisters can pray at intervals throughout the day. They will not return to the patients until prayers are over. For most medical people, this practice is hard to accept—nurses are notorious for getting urinary tract infections because they won't leave their patients long enough to go to the bathroom during a shift. But putting God first is a tenet of the Missionaries of Charity's faith, and I believe this dogged devotion to prayer, offering to God first and to man second, will perpetuate their order while others fade away.

From the first day, life in Kolkata tested the level of my tenacity, and I don't think I have what it would take to live as if I were poor in Kolkata. How do the Missionaries of Charity manage to sustain themselves in such difficult situations? Mother Teresa explained: "To be able to do this, our sisters, our lives have to be woven with prayer. They have to be woven with Christ to be able to understand, to share."[11] Constant rededication is what keeps them going. I'm in awe of Mother Teresa for adhering to this throughout her life, for always trusting that God would provide.

Mother Teresa seems to have had a tremendous capacity for trust, and I wish I had known her personally. Most of what I've learned about her has come from books. The faces of those who knew her reflect her joy when they speak of her, and in videos people flock to her, bowing their heads so that she can bless them. She greets them with a smile. In fact, the hallmark of her legacy is cheerfulness. Her spirit lingers in her facilities and the people who knew her. She said: "Smile at each other, make time for each other in your family. Smile at each other." And, if I had to choose one characteristic that I remember most about the Missionaries of Charity and their followers, it would be the smiles. They are luminous reflections of Mother Teresa's teachings.

The Missionaries of Charity refer to her simply as Mother, and it is easy to see that there will never be another Mother in their hearts. But once she was a girl named Agnes.

Agnes Gonxha Bojaxhiu was born to an Albanian Catholic family on August 26, 1910, in Skopje, Macedonia. She later chose to claim August 27 as her birthday, because that was her date of baptism.

I've seen pictures of her as a young girl, posing beside her sister in traditional Albanian dress. She reminds me of women I saw during my college days in the former Yugoslavia, when I traveled through Macedonia to the Albanian border.

In a childhood picture that hangs on the wall near her tomb, she is tiny and she wears the smile that was to become famous throughout the world. She looks like any little girl of eight, but her mind was already filled with weighty thoughts. She knew by the age of twelve that she wanted to dedicate her life to missionary work. At eighteen, she journeyed to Dublin, Ireland, where she became a postulate of the Sisters of Loreto, and two months later she arrived in Kolkata, the capital of West Bengal. Pictures of her at this time show a diminutive woman, dwarfed by her black and white nun's habit.

As a postulate in the Loreto community, she taught geography at Saint Mary's Bengali Medium School. Saint Mary's served the poor and also educated primary school teachers. In May 1931 Agnes became Sister Teresa, named for Saint Thérèse of Lisieux, the patron of missionaries.

There were similarities between Saint Thérèse and Mother Teresa. Saint Thérèse knew early on that she wanted to dedicate her life to God. Having received special permission from the Pope, she became a Carmelite nun at the age of fifteen. It was her philosophy that, when based upon childlike love and trust in God, small things could result in great good. She, like Mother Teresa, dedicated herself to being a servant to all, committed to achieving tasks that others saw as lowly. It is just these lowly tasks that bring dignity in the last days of terminal illness.

Many times I'd seen hospice patients admitted from the hospitals near the time of their deaths, filthy and withdrawn from the world around them. Shampooing the hair and cleaning the fingernails are lower priorities than life-sustaining measures in curative medicine, so those things often go undone in critical care units. At hospice, there is no higher priority than providing human dignity, so we immediately bathe, shampoo, and spruce-up our patients upon admission. I have personally soaked a patient's fingernails for half an hour to remove dried-in dirt. Surprisingly, once returned to their accustomed level of grooming, patients' spirits brighten, and they regain a modicum of control over the life that is slipping away. It helps them stop saying, "I don't want anyone to see me like this," and let's them spend their last moments with people they love—to live until they die. It was moments like that—the little victories—that made me happiest at hospice, so in that, I understand what she was saying.

Saint Thérèse became known as "The Little Flower." Among other reasons, she compared herself to a simple flower amidst the grassy floor of the forests. As she explained, people overlook the ordinary blooms, but even these mundane creations are pleasing to God. Not unlike Saint Thérèse, Mother Teresa saw herself as "a little pencil in God's hand" and insisted that she did nothing; God did it all.

Sister Teresa took her final vows in 1938 and continued to teach at the school until 1948. Hers was a cloistered existence, except when she traveled to and from the school. On these walks she watched as the world around her changed.

Even today in India, life and death, beauty and horror live openly side-by-side. Along with the architectural miracle of the Taj Mahal is the squalor of overcrowding that forces millions to live out their lives on the street. This contrast was even greater in colonial India, and the years 1943-1944 brought terrible famine to Bengal. Estimates are that, in 1943 alone, four million people died in the eastern part of India. In desperation, people poured into Kolkata from the countryside, and the waves of immigration that followed upset the balance of life in this, the secondary capital of the British Empire, for generations to come.

In the midst of all this turmoil, a new path became clear to Mother Teresa. On September 10, 1946, Mother was riding the train to Darjeeling when she had a revelation, "a call within a call," as she described it. "I realized that I had the call to take care of the sick and the dying, the hungry, the naked, the homeless—to be God's Love in action to the poorest of the poor."[12]

After that revelation, she asked permission to establish an order of nuns who would dedicate themselves to cheerfully serve those no one else wanted. She specified that the order's purpose would not be to build great institutions or to give charity to the poor. Instead, they would offer caring to the unwanted, because to Mother Teresa, not being wanted was the ultimate form of poverty. To illustrate this point, she often told the story of a woman she had rescued from the streets. This woman had been kicked out of her house by her own son and left to die from hunger and infected wounds that teemed with maggots. The woman cried but said she did not cry because of her wounds. She cried because her own family did not want her.

The Missionaries of Charity try to be family to those they serve, as well as those who work alongside them. Mother Teresa said: "Love begins at home, and it is not how much we do, but how much love we put in the action that we do."[13] She intended for her order to live that philosophy.

As Mother sought to establish the Missionaries, the world around her was changing. In 1947 India gained independence from the British Empire, and hundreds of thousands died in the violence that ensued. The Muslim people of what is now Pakistan sought independence from the Hindus of India. Bengal split into West Bengal and Bangladesh, with Bangladesh receiving the majority of the Muslims and West Bengal the majority of Hindus. This exceptionally violent war brought wave after wave of refugees into Kolkata, and death and dying pervaded the times.

On January 30, 1948, Mohandas Karamchand Gandhi—better known in the West as Mahatma Gandhi, which means "the great soul"—was assassinated by Hindu extremist Nauram Godse. Godse blamed Gandhi for allowing the Muslims to break away from India and form Pakistan.

The government in Kolkata attempted to house and feed the refugees for a while, but their efforts were soon defeated by the ever—increasing numbers of people seeking refuge from the hopelessness of life in the countryside. These people were already destitute and poorly nourished because of the famine. Disease thrived among them, and as the slums grew, hunger and despair followed. Kolkata's resources were overwhelmed and people died on the streets.

On August 18, 1948, Mother left the convent to dedicate her life to serving the poor, trading her Loreto habit for a white sari with a blue border. Possessing only eight rupees, she counted on God to provide what she needed to start an open-air school for the children in the slums. She was alone for less than a year when the first of those who would become her Missionaries of Charity, Sister Agnes, joined in her work.

In 1951 the first group of twelve sisters began their study to become Missionaries of Charity. By 1959 their numbers were large enough to establish their first missionary home outside Kolkata. In the 1960s, they were able to open homes in other nations, reaching Venezuela in 1965 and Tanzania in 1968. The Missionary Brothers of Charity were founded in 1963, and in 1984 the Lay Missionaries of Charity were born. The Lay Missionaries are single and married people who take vows of chastity within marriage, poverty, obedience, and service to the poor. The first of the Lay Missionaries took their vows in Rome in Mother Teresa's presence.

Today the Missionaries of Charity number in the thousands and operate more than six hundred facilities in over one hundred countries. In an era when the Catholic Church finds it difficult to recruit nuns, the Missionaries of Charity continue to grow.

Mother Teresa was conservative, and her stand on abortion and use of public forums to propagate this view has been criticized. But she didn't just preach; she took in abandoned children and mothers out-of-wedlock. When she spoke against abortion, she begged to be given unwanted children and pledged always to find room for them. Today in Kolkata alone there are several Missionaries of Charity homes that accept children.

The path her followers choose is not an easy one. They give up everything and follow strict rules in a life of service and contemplation. There are no modernized habits with street-length skirts and abbreviated headpieces. Everyone wears the sari, which goes atop a loose sheath. Only the face, hands, and sandaled feet are revealed. Their path is clear: cheerfully serve God and the poor—in that order. I think this demanding path, devoid of choices, is one of the reasons the Missionaries of Charity's numbers swell. There is no halfway, no worldly comfort that leaves one wanting just a little more.

Malcolm Muggeridge's 1969 BBC film and 1971 book, *Something Beautiful for God*, made Mother Teresa a world figure. She has, in fact, been criticized for becoming such a public person. Some saw her actions as self-aggrandizing, but I don't believe she wanted recognition for herself. She wanted to focus the world's attention on the plight of the poor and what could be done about it. Her fame drew volunteers and other resources that allowed her order to grow throughout the world, and little by little, one person at a time, they still work to diminish the suffering wherever they are.

Others have criticized her for associating with people of ill repute. The obvious rebuttal is that Jesus sought out sinners, but also, I don't think that a person's reputation would be of significance to her. After all, her goal was to reflect the light of Christ and not to decide who was worthy of her attentions. As it says in Luke 6:37-38: "Do not judge, and you will not be judged. Do not condemn, and you will not be condemned. Forgive, and you will be forgiven."

Mother Teresa won many awards, each of which she accepted in the name of the poor. In 1979 she won the Nobel Prize. When notified she said:

I accept the prize in the name of the poor. The prize is the recognition of the poor World. Jesus said, "I am hungry, I am naked, I am homeless." By serving the poor, I am serving Him.[14]

Though she accepted the prize, she refused the celebratory banquet, asking that the money—approximately $6,000—be given to those in need.

But with worldwide fame came more detractors. Some said that she forced her religion on others, demanding conversion and secretly baptizing people against their will. I never saw the slightest hint of this in Kolkata, nor among the sisters in the U.S. In fact, Mother herself said:

> There is only one God and He is God to all; therefore it is important that everyone is seen as equal before God. I've always said we should help a Hindu become a better Hindu, a Muslim become a better Muslim, a Catholic become a better Catholic. We believe our work should be our example to people. We have among us 475 souls—30 families are Catholics and the rest are all Hindus, Muslims, Sikhs—all different religions. But they all come to our prayers.[15]

In 1982 she visited war-torn Beirut, where she heard that a hospital for mentally disabled children was caught in the crossfire. So powerful was her influence by that time, she was able to ask for and receive a cease-fire between the Israelis and Palestinians that lasted long enough for her to rescue those children.

By 1983 her health was deteriorating. It was that year when she suffered her first heart attack. In 1989 she had another heart attack and received a pacemaker. Still, she did not slow down. In the years that followed, she continued to meet her own harsh standards and was hospitalized with episodes of pneumonia and heart failure as she traveled about the world.

After naming Sister Nirmala to be her successor, Mother Teresa stepped down as head of the order in March 1997, and with her cardiac condition then complicated by malaria, she died on September 5, 1997. Over fifty years of working for the poor had taken its toll. Interestingly, she died almost one hundred years to the date after Saint Thérèse, who died on September 30, 1897.

On October 19, 2003, she was officially made a saint. At the beatification, Pope John Paul II said:

> A Missionary of Charity: this is what Mother Teresa was in name and in fact...A missionary of charity, a missionary of peace, a

missionary of life...A missionary with the most universal language: the language of love that knows no bounds or exclusion
and has no preferences other than for the most forsaken.[16]

This is why I wanted to know more about her work and her followers. What I found was more simple and profound than I had imagined. It
took me a while to stop viewing things through my own culture, religion,
and training. Because of that, I had initial questions about why things were
done as they were, but in the end I began to see the logic in the choices
made. So to the detractors I say, if you can do a better job, get out there
and do it. No one would be more thankful for your work than the Missionaries of Charity.

EARLY ONE MORNING

At two-forty in the morning I was awakened by the mother of all rainstorms. Weighty drops pummeled the corrugated metal roofs beneath my window. At times it sounded as if someone were training a fire hose across the metal, lifting portions then slamming them down. Lightning ripped across the sky and thunder punctuated the churning sounds of water that surged along the roof and alleyways. I'd heard that such storms were episodic, ceasing as abruptly as they began, so I listened and waited.

Though my bed was a sturdy frame with wooden slats covered by a surprisingly comfortable spring-less mattress, the thunder actually caused it to shake like tremors I'd felt during minor earthquakes in northern California. Amid this impressive demonstration of nature's power, I wondered what was happening to the people sleeping on the streets.

A couple of men shouted to each other in Hindi as they ran past my door, and I remembered the window at the end of the hall was always open, save for the grates. No doubt the rain was pouring in and they had come to shut it.

Suddenly, I remembered that I had not brought an umbrella, since I'd specifically timed my trip to avoid the rainy season. Taking stock of my wardrobe, I decided that sandals and a dark batik Punjabi shirt were my best choices for rain attire. The material was the heaviest cotton I had and the shirt covered me to mid-shin, which would hide the lightweight white trousers that went with it.

At three o'clock the storm continued unabated, and I worried that the gutters were disgorging opaque brown water onto the streets and side-walks. I'd seen pictures of Kolkatans wading through such muck during the rainy season, and of course, foremost on my mind were the medical implications. Where people come in contact with water that has mixed with human waste, there is always a chance of cholera—the deadly diarrhea disease that lurks in areas where sanitation is poor. Without treatment, it kills quickly. I wondered how to tell the difference between early stages of cholera and traveler's diarrhea or food poisoning. Checking myself into a hospital would be a last resort after all I'd read about them. Meanwhile, the non-nurse side of me worried about something more mundane: since many who live on the sidewalks use the streets as latrines, what would it be like walking through murky waters and not being able to see what lay beneath? Heightening my apprehension was the thought of the razor blades that littered the sidewalks where men had been bathing and shaving.

One thing became clear as the downpour raged on: I was glad to be living on the second floor of a hotel with my windows tightly closed. Had I stayed at Monica House as originally planned, I would have been sleeping on the ground floor, with the windows and doors open for ventilation, battling mosquitoes and God knows what else. At least at the Circular I felt safe. One of the waiters at the Oberoi had warned me it would not be safe to venture out alone at night—as if that thought had not occurred to me. All I could say was "Don't worry. Kolkata is intimidating enough by day."

Speaking of safety, there were no volunteers taking the bus back to the Mother House after yesterday's morning shift, because they were all going out to eat. I didn't want to join them because I had to attend a meeting at the Mother House at three o'clock that afternoon and hadn't slept well the night before. It seemed like the best choice to forgo lunch and return to my hotel to rest for a little while.

There are at least four different buses that stop within walking distance of the Circular, but some are dreadfully slow because they make so many stops. I just didn't know which was which, so I decided to negotiate a prepaid price with one of the cabs parked along a side street near the Kali Temple. The scene that ensued topped my previous taxi escapade.

First, the cabby badgered me until I agreed to a price that was beyond what I knew the standard fare to be. Even though he was swindling me, I couldn't blame the guy. The extra money meant nothing more than pennies and principle to me, and I figured he'd see my potential as a regular customer and drive me home safely. But customer service is not a firm concept in Kolkata cabbyland. This bleary-eyed guy drove me miles away from where I needed to be, all the while smoking what smelled like marijuana. He then dropped me off God knows where, saying the Mother House was around the corner. By the time he told me to get out of the cab, I was more than ready to escape, but the Mother House was not "just around the corner" where he said it would be.

I asked a woman for help, and she sent me off one hundred and eighty degrees opposite my original path. After a block, I decided to double-check and asked a man to help. He pointed to the direction from which I'd come. I took one more chance when I encountered a man who spoke English. I handed him my letter of invitation from the Missionaries of Charity, so he could read the address and not mistake where I wanted to go because of mispronunciations.

A crowd gathered, with everyone standing too close for comfort, pointing in different directions, and speaking all at once in accents I had trouble understanding. A feeling of desperation was rising in me when an Indian man in a polo helmet drove up on a motorcycle and said the Mother House was too far to reach on foot. Would I like to come with him?

A quick look around convinced me I didn't want to stay where I was or brave the gauntlet on the sidewalk, and though it makes no sense in the retelling that I found this alternative more inviting, I hopped on the back of the motorcycle and off we went. He was right. It was very far.

Navigating through Kolkata traffic is like making your way through a swarm of bees, especially for an American who's used to traffic keeping to the right. In India, it is on the left—mostly—but that all changes when someone attempts to make lanes where there are none. It is horrific in a car, but on a motorcycle without a helmet, it is beyond reason. As we sped away, I realized that I couldn't wrap my arms around this man because he might think it a come-on. So, I tightened my abdominal muscles to hold my body straight and tried to hold onto the edges of the slender seat.

I didn't make a peep when a cab grazed my leg, opening a shallow but long gash and almost knocking us to the ground. Everywhere we turned we encountered traffic jams. At one vehicular snarl, he spotted a policeman who was sort of directing cars and gave him a hand signal. The cop nodded, and—to my horror—we took off the wrong way down a major road.

By this time I was beyond worry and into hysteria. The problem became how to suppress nervous giggles while I tried to keep my balance without touching the driver. In the end, the man was honorable and took me to the Mother House via a fairly direct route.

When we stopped, I offered him money but he refused, looking insulted. I thanked him profusely and hurried toward the Mother House, where the sari-clad sisters had literally rolled up their sleeves and had a fire-bucket brigade going on, passing great bags of rice—probably fifty pounds each—from group to group to haul inside. They said they didn't need my help, so I jaywalked across traffic alongside a man herding long-eared, bleating goats, then ran to the hotel. I already knew that the "walk" light on the traffic signal was just a ploy to lure pedestrians into complacency, so they'd be off guard when a car came zooming through the crosswalk.

I reached my room with half the grit of Kolkata caked to my body. The cut on my leg had bled through my white pants, so I cleaned it with the antiseptic wipes I'd packed in my suitcase. I knew I had to take care of this wound, since infections fester in the tropics. Also, I was taking care of patients who were afflicted with the highly infectious bacterium *Pseudomonas* and heaven knows what else. I didn't need to expose an open wound needlessly.

As I undressed, I found that the letter from the Missionaries of Charity I'd carried in my money belt, along with my money and other papers, were soaked with sweat. The papers were falling apart and the ink had run. So much for the U.S. Department of State's advice for American citizens to carry a copy of their passports at all times.

From that point forward, if it didn't fit in my pockets, I wouldn't carry it. My passport remained locked in the Circular's safe, and once the copy that lay in soggy shreds on my bed dried, I stored it in my suitcase. No more money belt.

By three-thirty, the torrent had subsided to persistent tapping, and the thunder growled like distant jets. I couldn't believe it, but the honking from the streets had begun anew. How many road obstructions could there have been to honk at that hour in a deluge?

I turned on the air-conditioning and it sounded like rocks were flying around inside the motor. I half expected it to spit them onto the bed but

I was too tired to care. Suddenly, the motor ground to a halt, so I turned it off and used the fan instead. The room stayed cool enough with the air agitating around me anyway, and the chocolate brown paddles of the fan whirled and purred above my head, lulling me back to sleep. The ceiling fixture shook rhythmically back and forth as it spun. Somewhere outside a dog barked.

As I drifted off to sleep, I wondered why the world was so rife with inequity. Why is my life good, while others struggle to survive? I believe that God is merciful and that Jesus took our sins upon the cross. I also believe that God is not so exclusive that he wishes for those who don't read the Bible the way I do to suffer. Yet thousands of children are born HIV positive and will die orphans when their parents die of AIDS. Across the globe, young girls are forced to be sex workers. Women are beaten and burned by their husbands, and families starve.

I'm no saint. I've "earned" no special considerations in this life, and yet I know that I've gotten them. My life has not always been happy. I've had two abusive marriages because I refused to see the reality that someone who says he loves you can actually get gratification from hurting you. I still suffer from periods of nightmares about the abuse. The funny thing is that even knowing what I know about people, I can still be a bit of a doormat. On the whole, however, I'd still rather forgive too much than too little.

The men and women who come to *Kalighat* are life's discards. They are beaten and battered. Even if they heal and return home, it will not be to a life I'd wish for myself, yet despite all that, when I see their faces in my mind, they are smiling. We laughed all day at *Kalighat*, even though we shared no common language, and, during some of the most terrible bandage changes of my nursing career, patients thanked me.

A big part of it is the sisters. When you look into the face of one who wants nothing from you, who is smiling and open and wants to be near you just because you are, you can't help but be happy. When I'm with them, the ugliness of this world fades away. How much I want to keep that feeling and share it with others for the rest of my life.

I've had so many "important" jobs. I sat on a Presidential national security advisory committee on information technology. People listened when I spoke. I felt significant. Yet I now realize there is loss in the grand achievements of life. All you get from achievement is thirst for more and disappointment if you can't surpass it the next time. The heart has more to gain from the simple labors of the hand. Who doesn't look back on life and see that the things that matter are the things you did with loved ones—for parents, those late night moments holding your babies in your arms and looking into their sweet faces as they wet all over you? Would you give that up? I wouldn't.

The interesting thing is that the "lowly" caregiver tasks tend to be relegated to women; yet caregiving can be the most rewarding experience of all. In the U.S., women strive for equality and shun the work of making life good for others—the cooking, cleaning, diaper changing. I know I did. I pushed myself to achieve my career goals. I was one of the first hundred women to become an FBI agent, and one of the first female supervisors at FBI headquarters. I received eight commendations from directors of the FBI, even one from the director of the Secret Service. Those letters are stuck in a scrapbook somewhere and, believe me, they are not the thoughts that soothe my soul in the depths of despair. At the time, they meant so much. Now I'd rather reclaim the time I missed with my children while I was out earning recognition.

They were young—Chris six and Kendra two—when I joined the FBI in 1977. I was a single parent. My first assignment was fugitives and background investigations, but I met a woman from the counterterrorism squad and began to work undercover against remnants of the Weather Underground in San Francisco's barrio. We had to quit when our suspects posted notices that "the women of the FBI" were sleuthing around the barrio. Fearing that the subjects of our investigation had booby-trapped the door to our undercover apartment, the bomb techs cleared the room for us, but it didn't make sense to go back with our covers blown. It was an exciting ending to a dreary surveillance, but it sparked my interest in counterterrorism work.

The hours were long, but the work was fun, even if it was extremely difficult to make it as one of the first hundred women. When I'd been in the field only a few months, a supervisor came to my house late at night under the ruse that he needed to talk to me about an undercover case. The problem was, he was referring to the covers of my bed. He was drunk and took his clothes off while I was in another room, then chased me around the living-room a couple of rounds until I was finally able to get him to go. My children were asleep in a nearby room and stayed that way, thank God. I went into work the next day and asked a senior agent what I should do about the incident. It was then I learned what I was to learn again and again in the FBI: I could either keep my mouth shut or get out, because fight though I would, I was not going to beat the system. As a twenty-seven-year-old single parent who had a job that would support her children well and the hope that this man was an exception to the rule, I decided to keep my mouth shut.

As I clawed my way along, I worked long hours, hoping to get beyond the woman-thing and be viewed on equal standing with the other agents. Many accepted me, but many did not. I tried hard to ignore it and just do my job. Casework came easy to me and I earned success, eventually supervising an international counterterrorism program at FBI headquarters, then a joint terrorism task force of FBI, Secret Service, Immigration and Naturalization, and several police departments in the field. As my thirteen years as an agent unfolded, the pettiness began to wear on me. Worst of all, I took the daily slurs to heart and felt diminished. Though I sank into depression, I managed to hide it from most people outside my family. On the job, depression came out as anger, which was perfectly acceptable in the FBI world. All it did was bolster my reputation of being tough. Go figure.

At home, I was just sad. My children suffered not only from my long hours, but also from a mother who came home drained and listless. I thought I had failed everyone when I left the Bureau, but in fact, I had won. It was a victory that I could turn my back on a good pension and the glory I always got from successful casework. In the end, my life has been richer for giving up prideful and lofty accomplishments.

I will never understand how anyone can take joy in hurting another, but India had given me new perspective. It did not make me feel better to know that others suffered incomprehensibly more than I. Instead, Kolkata had helped me appreciate the truly important tasks of life—the simple things that don't make the headlines but mean the world to just one person.

The last thought I recall before I closed my eyes that night, was that I wanted to keep my focus on good things for the rest of my life. Kolkata had given me a special gift—a clearer vision of what makes life worthwhile. Still, I wondered: Have I learned this lesson enough to live by it, or will I backslide when I return to the world of shopping malls and important business?

At four forty-two I sat bolt upright, startled from a deep sleep. The

Muslim prayers had begun. Unfortunately, the traffic and its concomitant honking almost drowned out the prayers. Within five minutes, a chorus of calls to prayer projected through loudspeakers from different directions around the neighborhood. A dog howled along with them.

I was reminded of a tale told to me by a State Department Diplomatic Security Service officer who had a heavy New Jersey accent. Early in his career he was on a protective detail, which took him to the Middle East for the first time in his life. Suffering from jet lag, he had just fallen asleep when the call to prayers began. Incensed by the noise, he threw open a window and shouted, "Would you hold it down out there? I'm trying to get some sleep!"

At that moment, I felt his pain.

BEING PART OF SOMETHING GOOD

Anjali did not speak. She lay curled on her cot in the fetal position, knees held tight to her chest by encircling arms no wider than my wrists. Beaten and raped, she had been brought in from Kolkata's Howrah train station during the night.

Her eyes were swollen shut, and a great gash ran from just below her shaven hairline, through the left brow, and into the bony orbit of her left eye. Her lips protruded in a cockeyed manner that told me her assailant had hit her there too.

As I approached her cot, light streamed through the window, spilling onto the mahogany curves of her baby face. She was most likely in her early to mid-teens—more than a decade younger than my own daughter. No one could determine her exact age, because the few words she had spoken were tribal, and no one in *Kalighat* spoke her language. Despite the communications barrier, I had to conduct the admitting exam.

The sutures in Angali's forehead were of crude string. Someone at the train station had stitched her up with what was on hand. Luckily, there was no sign of infection along the joined edges of the facial wound, and the sutures were intact. This was all I could see without touching her.

My most difficult task was to determine whether her genitals required stitches, and if so, to suture her. I wanted to approach her slowly and make her as comfortable as possible. After all, she could not see me through her bulbous eyelids and certainly could not understand what I was saying. I had no idea how she'd react to an exam, having just been raped. All I could do was try to win her over with gentle words.

As kindly as I could, I talked to her, to let her hear that I was approaching. Then I sat down on her cot but didn't touch her. Touching a rape victim without permission does not necessarily provide comfort, and I knew Anjali had had enough assumptions made about her body.

After a few minutes of what I hoped were soothing words and a couple of test pats on the arm, Anjali lay silent and stiff but did not fight me. With forty-nine other patients awaiting care, I had to conduct the exam, even though she was not yet relaxed. At least she was accustomed to my voice. I lifted her skirt and took a quick peek, describing what I was doing and why, just to help her understand that it was me examining her. She didn't fight me. She didn't even move. I had a good view because she had been bathed clean and because of the position she froze into while I was sitting on her cot.

I could see no obvious external injury. No blood, bruising, or swelling, or external signs of sexually transmitted disease. I decided to spare her the vaginal exam for the time being.

For the next part of the exam I'd have to touch her, so I sat back down on the cot, this time with her back to me. Resting my hand on her arm, I laid my stethoscope on her upper back where the gown had fallen open. As I moved my stethoscope in a zigzag pattern down either side of her spine to compare the sound at the same points in each lung, I was relieved to hear nothing abnormal. At least there was no obvious tuberculosis such as I'd seen in so many patients in the few days I'd been at *Kalighat*.

Her heart rate was seventy beats per minute and regular—well within normal ranges—and her abdomen was soft, which meant there was no internal hemorrhage, intestinal problem, urinary retention, enlarged organs, or months-old pregnancy that I could feel under the pressure of my hands. Her skin felt cool with no elevation of temperature, which gave me hope that she might be infection-free. Of course, heaven only knew what was incubating in her system.

Other than the results of the beating, the exam was normal; but likely as not, she'd been exposed to a sexually transmitted disease. And she was probably in pain.

Concluding the exam, I decided on antibiotics and pain control as the initial treatments. The antibiotics would fight sexually transmitted disease and help prevent that slash across her face from festering in the tropical environment.

Capsules and water in hand, I returned to Anjali's side and perched on the cot beside her, trying not to crowd. A white-clad novice sat on the other side, explaining in Bengali—the major language spoken in Kolkata—why I thought the pills were necessary.

Anjali's lips fell slightly ajar, so I pressed the antibiotic into her mouth. I let her feel the cup of water near her lips before I poured. Suddenly, her jaws clamped shut. She flailed wildly at me and kicked her feet, then spit out the medicine. Instinctively, I caught the precious antibiotic capsule in my ungloved hand. We didn't have an endless supply.

I asked the novice to help me reassure Anjali that we weren't going to hurt her. The novice, little more than a teen herself, spoke in a calm tone while Anjali lay rigid. My hand rested on Anjali's arm, where I felt the underlying muscles. Her nutrition was poor and the muscles felt slack, not elastic and vital like the arms of my own children.

We tried again to give the capsule, speaking soothingly and patting her hand. This time Anjali spit the partially dissolved substance onto my Punjabi shirt, and I had to scrape the gummy mess off my chest.

What caused this sudden change? Why could I examine her genitals without a fight, but not give her antibiotics or pain pills? Had someone forced drugs on her? As young as she was, I wondered whether she were a prostitute or whether she had been sexually abused so many times that she no longer protested people touching her intimate parts.

Concerned that the girl would develop a sexually transmitted disease, the novice wanted me to give her an injected antibiotic. The idea was medically sound, but I thought Anjali had been traumatized enough. Antibiotic serums are thick and have a large volume, so they don't inject quickly. If she struggled, I'd probably end up damaging her tissues and really hurting her. I wanted to give her a day to get used to her surroundings and realize she was not in danger before I jabbed her with needles she couldn't see coming.

Maybe she'd feel more at ease with us in the morning. Maybe her eyes would open, at least a slit.

I wished I could consult a doctor, but there would be none that day. A local volunteer doctor conducted rounds on Sundays and Wednesdays, so I'd have to wait a few more days. Rarely, other doctors floated through, but most of the time the responsibility for diagnosis and deciding on treatment rested with the nurses and the sisters. The reality in the Third World is that you have two choices as a nurse: do what you can for a patient, or watch them suffer and die. The luxury of calling a doctor, discussing your assessment and what you think would be an appropriate treatment, then getting an order as we do in the United States, wasn't an option at *Kalighat.*

Patients were brought in off the street in emergency conditions. Most had no lab tests or imagery to help determine first care actions—perhaps in a day or two these could be obtained, but not immediately.

I soon began to appreciate my Johns Hopkins training, which they dubbed "nursing school on the medical school model." The course was geared toward preparing us to enter masters-level nurse practitioner programs, and since the role of nurse practitioners is often comparable to that of family doctors, we were taught physical assessment, pharmacology, and thinking through what we saw, heard, smelled, and felt during physical exams. I never realized how much I knew until I had to rely so profoundly upon myself without the backup of a medical doctor.

Not all nurses are taught assessment in such depth, though many pick it up through experience. I was astounded to find that one of the best nurses I encountered at *Kalighat* had never been taught how to listen to a chest. In some countries only doctors are allowed to insert urinary catheters, but in most Western countries, nursing responsibilities have advanced far beyond what most people think of as nursing. With proper credentials, RNs such as woundcare specialists can perform minor surgeries. Advanced practice nurses can perform minor surgeries and prescribe medications. We've come a long way since the days my mother describes in the 1940s when nurses had to call a resident to take a blood pressure.

Because I used a stethoscope, the rumor went around *Kalighat* that I was really a doctor, and I couldn't disabuse some of the people of this impression. All I could do was shake my head and correct them when they called me doctor, but with my law enforcement background, the situation unnerved me because it smacked of impersonation.

Eventually, volunteers and even some of the sisters came to me for medical advice. When I protested that I was not a doctor, one of them said to me, "You might as well be." In the end I gave up. I listened to their symptoms, examined them as best I could, and told them what I would do for myself if I had the same medical complaint.

I had an especially hard time accepting that I was practicing in a place where the laws and traditions of the United States didn't exist. Everything from the nursing floor to the pharmacies was different. As I said before, in India, you don't have to have a prescription for non-narcotic drugs, including psychiatric medications. You just go to the chemist and ask for what you want.

In the West, nursing floors are organized to help avoid errors, but even under the best of circumstances it is impossible to be error-free. The reason is that healthcare workers are just a bunch of human beings doing the best they can with what they have. Compound this with patients whose state of health, pain, and genetics make them react differently from the expected norm to medications and procedures, and the inevitable result is caregiver stress and mistakes.

At *Kalighat*, I felt the added pressure of having to answer multiple questions—sometimes not in my native language or through an interpreter—while drawing up injections, calculating doses without the benefit of a pharmacist, trying to find a medication that would substitute for what they didn't have, or trying to figure out what to do for a medical condition I'd never encountered before. *Kalighat* adds to this mix of potential pitfalls: nurses trained in different traditions, volunteers who want to help but don't have medical training, a patient-to-nurse ratio that is sometimes fifty or one hundred to one, plus patients with mental illness, severe disease, and no full-time or on-call doctor. All this made nursing difficult, but when it worked and people improved, it was worth every bit of the worry.

That night I awakened at three o'clock—a factor of anxiety paired with the ten-hour time difference between Kolkata and the East Coast of the United States. However, I was getting used to fragmented sleep and tried to look on it as a time to reflect.

As I thought about the day, I realized it had been hard, but there were also moments of peace and bliss. After I finished the bandage changes that morning, I'd stopped to drink a cup of tea. *Kalighat*'s balcony has a small niche where there is just enough room for one or two people to stand. When I stepped out onto it, its walls shielded me from the other volunteers' conversations and from my worries over the wounds and disease downstairs. Humidity plumped the air, but the slight breeze bore a spicy fragrance that soothed me as I sipped my tea and looked out over the bazaar in the street below.

Shopkeepers' pallets and stands lined the dusty road. Their patrons—some richly dressed, some clothed only in loincloths—strolled among them. A few of the people on the street were emaciated, but most looked relatively well fed, even among the beggars. The splashes of colorful flowers and textile displays broke the monotony of the soot and grime.

A huge crow, black with a gray ring around its neck, stared at me from the balcony railing. He picked at a crust of bread, cocking his head from side to side to view me from different vantage points, while automobile horns honked in angry cacophony in the distance.

Again, I pondered what had brought me to Kolkata. Opportunities slide by in life, yet we seize so few. Why did I choose this one? Was it just a hospice nursing adventure? An exploration of faith? Of culture? Or an attempt to shake myself from lethargy, from a life too comfortable, expected? Eighteenth-century Scottish philosopher Edmund Burke said, "Evil triumphs when good men do nothing," and I have always believed that if you do nothing about community problems, you have no right to complain. This was the reason I made the trip. I wasn't thinking I could change the world, but I was hoping to make the days go better for a small portion of its population.

I remember a scene from the movie *Sylvia*, which recounts the life story of poet Sylvia Plath. She described her life as a tree. Each branch represented a different path; each leaf a different choice. But she couldn't decide which choice to make, and the leaves dried up and blew away. I guess I am her opposite—impulsive enough to grab now and think later.

As I leaned against the balcony wall, I realized how tired I was. I'd been working for hours without a break, bent over to reach the women on the shin-high cots. I felt exhausted, hardly able to move; yet in that moment there was perfection and peace like I'd rarely felt in my life. Everything that had happened, the fears for my safety, the treachery of cab drivers, and the confusion on the nursing floor melted in the haze. In that moment, I knew that I was part of something good.

OUTREACH OF HOPE

"Whatever you do to the least of my brothers, that you do unto me" is a song the sisters sing. It is based upon Christ's words about helping the poor, and the tune has become stuck in my head. We sang this song at least once a shift to remind ourselves why we were there. But this day was my day off and I planned not to work at all.

Mother Teresa's volunteers work either mornings, afternoons or both, except on Thursdays, which are enforced volunteer days off. There is no required commitment of time and no special qualification needed to volunteer, so everyone can contribute something. In our orientation, the sisters explained that we should not feel forced or obligated; if we didn't feel like coming in, we should not. At our worksites, we were to do only what we felt comfortable doing. Our days would not be orchestrated. Our work was to come from the heart.

Volunteers could serve at several Missionaries of Charity centers in and around Kolkata, and nurses and doctors could attend the mobile dispensaries by invitation of the sisters. Specialized dispensaries, such as gynecology and neurology, were held in the courtyard of the *Shishu Bhavan* home for unwanted and abandoned children nearest the Mother House. On other days the sisters rode around the countryside and set up at various sites to treat whoever was in need. They conducted exams, applied first aid, and distributed medications. People could bring in notes from doctors or hospitals, and if the sisters had the medication on hand, they'd give it to them without cost.

Among the Missionaries of Charity facilities in and around Kolkata is *Nabo Jibon*, which is located across the Hugli River in an area of Howrah known as the "City of Joy." This home serves multiple purposes and accepts virtually anyone in medical need, ranging from tuberculosis to men with physical and mental handicaps to geriatrics and malnourished children.

Prem Dan, which means "to give love," is a long-term care setting. It was established after the numbers of people who got better in *Kalighat* swelled. Over sixty percent of the patients who are admitted to *Kalighat* recover. When they are well enough to leave *Kalighat* but not to return to their families or the streets, they are transferred to *Prem Dan*. Many *Prem Dan* patients have mental disabilities.

Shishu Bhavan means "children's home," and there is more than one of these. One *Shishu Bhavan* houses toddlers and babies with mental and physical handicaps, along with children who are expected to be adopted. Only female volunteers are allowed there, although I never found out why. A second *Shishu Bhavan* was set up for children who are not expected to be adopted. Both male and female volunteers are accepted there.

Daya Dan means "to give kindness." This home takes in children, ages eight through thirteen, who have mental and physical handicaps. Many blind children live there, as well as many with neurological problems, which often resulted from head trauma during difficult births.

The leper colony at Titagarh is called the *Gandhiji Prem Nivas*, meaning "Gandhi's gift of love" to honor Gandhi's work with lepers. *Prem Nivas* is different from the other facilities in that they manufacture textile goods. Mother realized that the disease of leprosy is easy to treat, but the broken soul that goes with being ostracized by society is not. She understood that these people suffer not only from financial poverty, but a poverty of hope, and this she and her sisters set out to remedy.

To build self-respect and sufficiency, the people of *Prem Nivas* are taught to hand-make textiles. They produce the sheets that are used in Mother's Kolkata facilities and also weave the materials for the sisters' saris. Hundreds of people live in the *Prem Nivas* community, which stretches for ten kilometers along the Titagarh-Khardah railway line, and anyone can drop in for medications and bandage changes.

One Thursday, we walked for forty-five minutes to visit *Shanti Dan*, a former prison, where we had tea and lunch and discussion. *Shanti Dan*, which means "to give peace," houses small children and women with mental and physical disabilities. Many have been drug-addicted. *Shanti Dan* can accommodate up to two hundred people and accepts female volunteers only. The women there need social attention and personal care, such as conversation and help with their nails and other grooming. Such things build self-esteem and make the women feel accepted.

The discussion was led by a Jesuit priest I'll call Father Ignatius. Father Ignatius was in his sixties and had longish gray hair. His sandals were floppy and falling apart as he walked. I could count at least ten places in which his shirt had been darned, and his baggy gray pants were frayed at the cuff. While the pants stayed up, some of the belt loops had broken loose, and his belt was askew.

He taught physics at Kolkata's Xavier College, which was named for Saint Frances Xavier, a Basque missionary priest who cared for the poor and sick in many countries, including India, where he landed in 1542. He followed in the path of other Christians, such as the Apostle Thomas—also known as Doubting Thomas—who, tradition has it, was killed in India circa 72 A.D. It is said that he helped build a palace for King Gondophares, or Guduphara, who then ruled Afghanistan and what is today the Indian Punjab. Scholars argue whether this history of Saint Thomas is true, and that is just the sort of topic we addressed with Father Ignatius during the day of learning at *Shanti Dan*.

The discussion was intense, exploring topics such as "Why are we here on earth?" and "Could 2+2=5?" He guided our debate with great relish. A lover of philosophy, Father Ignatius posed questions but didn't answer them. Instead, he posited arguments and cited examples, hoping we would join in.

Jason Pittelli, a Canadian in his early twenties, matched Father Ignatius point for point. Tall and athletic, he had been working as a tour guide in the Vatican for part of the year while he considered options—finish his divinity studies or have more adventures. He had a great sense of humor but appeared contemplative at the same time.

Jason's experiences in Kolkata were different from mine. He walked more freely about the city and got to know more people than I, but he'd learned some hard lessons. He told me about a child he played with at a shop he frequented. He was shocked to learn one day that the boy he'd been playing with was not the owner's son but a child who'd been purchased for three hundred rupees—about seven U.S. dollars—per month. The money was being sent to the child's family and the child served at the shopkeeper's whim.

Most of the volunteers were young, and I was impressed with how they could take on the challenges of India, poverty, and profound illness. Jason was a case in point: at *Kalighat*, he treated the patients with great kindness, facing situations that would have been a challenge for anyone at any age. One day as I was making my way to the hand-washing station, our paths crossed. He was smiling and joking with a friend. Between them they carried a patient on a stretcher, whom they were transporting to the shower. The next time I saw Jason he looked a bit stunned. When I asked what was wrong, he told me the man he'd taken to the shower had died just as they'd put him back in bed. This kind of thing happened every day in *Kalighat*. For me, as a hospice nurse, it was almost an expectation in the cycle of life. But I am also more than fifty years old. I have lost friends and family and have had plenty of time to ponder what happens at the end of life. I wonder, though, how I would have faced it thirty years ago. Would I have had the strength to keep going back to *Kalighat* day after day?

This day of philosophical discussions also brought practical advice in the form of a message from Mother. Knowing her days were drawing to a close, she had asked Father Ignatius to pass on words of counsel. She said that seeing volunteers from all over the world made her happy, and she wanted us to be happy in Kolkata. She knew that patients are touched in profound ways when people from other countries care for them, especially since they've experienced rejection from their own countrymen.

She also left warnings about the realities of this wondrous, cruel place. She recommended that volunteers guard their belongings by carrying money and passports in front of the body, instead of in back where pickpockets can work without attracting attention. She counseled men and women alike never to accept food or drink from a stranger, because volunteers had been drugged, and women transported to other Indian cities and repeatedly raped. Even a priest was kidnapped and robbed after accepting a drug-laced cookie in a train station. She also said that if someone approaches on the street and offers to do something for you that you have not requested, say, "Thank you, but no." The people who were drugged had accepted food from those who offered unsolicited help.

Her final guidance was not to worry whether patients understand your words; they understand your actions. People will see God more clearly in what you do than in what you say.

After imparting these admonitions, Father Ignatius surveyed the room for topics volunteers wanted to discuss. When this round went on too long, an Irish volunteer, a woman who has been with the missionaries for years, chided him, "Father, I think we've had enough questions." He looked at her like a boy whose mother had said he had to stop playing baseball and come in for bed, but he stopped soliciting questions.

Throughout the day I'd been watching a group of half a dozen Japanese and Korean teens. They seemed to have varying levels of English skills, and two of the Japanese had hand-held translation devices. These teens were cheerful, yet demure, the girls shyly covering their mouths when they laughed and lowering their eyes when spoken to. Though each of them wore the Miraculous Medals they'd been given by the sisters when they signed up to volunteer, one of them told the group he did not believe in God. He only spoke a little English, so he could not engage in any complex explanation of his beliefs, but he exemplified the fact that people of all creeds are welcomed and respected at Mother Teresa's.

After the discussion and lunch, we toured *Shanti Dan*'s grounds. As I met the women who lived there, I realized that they probably had a better quality of life at this former prison than in their own homes.

While progress has been made toward women's rights in India, it is still the tradition among many families that the woman gets the leftovers, if there are any. Girls are viewed as an expense and boys as a gift. Female children may be raised eating only after the boys are satisfied. Theirs is a life of sacrifice, an ultimate form of which is the practice of *sati*, wherein the widow throws herself on the husband's funeral pyre. The custom is attributed to the Hindu religion but may have been imported from Scythia. It has been banned several times since the 1800s, with *The Commission of Sati (Prevention) Act* passed in 1987. The practice still has not died completely in rural areas.

At *Shanti Dan*, one woman's face had been so badly burned that it appeared to have melted, as if wax had dripped in sheets down a candlestick, leaving a rippled finish. Her mouth, which was permanently open and now a part of her neck, lacked a chin because her lower lip was fused to her chest. She came up to Father Ignatius and crouched on the ground before him, laying her forehead to his feet. When she stood up, she placed her hands together in the traditional *namaskar* pose and bowed to each of us as a greeting of peace. It was an emotionally shattering experience for me and I could hardly choke back the tears. Once again I'd seen how a simple act of love from a person who wants no glory could outshine what the world sees as great deeds.

Next, we walked a short way to a Missionaries of Charity AIDS hospice, where people lay in rows in the heat. No one spoke, though the room was crowded. Most were asleep. It was unusual in Mother Teresa's facilities not to see people chatting amongst themselves. Maybe they just didn't feel sociable in the heat of the day or maybe the ravages of disease had sapped their strength.

Next came a home for children with TB, but as usual, there was no protective gear for visitors. A tall, reed-thin Japanese girl, in her early twenties, entered a room of infants and leaned down at the side of a baby's crib. As the child lay listlessly with his eyes open, she talked to him and touched his little hand. This was a very sick baby, and while the girl was making a lovely gesture, I knew she had not understood the warning about TB or she wouldn't have gotten so close to the baby's face. TB is an airborne disease organism. I could do nothing about the fact that she had breathed infectious air into her lungs, but I made her use some of my antibacterial hand sanitizer when we left the room. Antibacterials won't prevent TB, but I hoped it would keep her from picking up other diseases that this immunosuppressed child's system might be harboring.

The visit ended on an uplifting note, when we went to *L'Arche*, a Canadian home for people with mental retardation. *L'Arche* is not connected with Mother Teresa, except that Mother Teresa donated the land their Kolkata facility is built on. I found the *L'Arche* community to be charming, to say the least.

I'm always amazed how people with Down's syndrome look like they come from the same family, no matter what the nationality; plus, they are universally the most loving humans on earth. I bought handmade greeting cards. The artists were all mentally handicapped, yet they even made the paper the cards were printed on.

As we walked, they crowded around and hugged us, introducing themselves and asking our names. The manager, an Indian national, tried to tell them some of our names but became flustered when he couldn't remember those of us he'd met. He gave me an embarrassed grin and said in a low voice, "I'm sorry, but Europeans look alike to me, and I can't tell you apart."

The *L'Arche* compound hinted at what Kolkata could be. Lush tropical plants, landscaped yellow-gold stuccoed buildings. Also, in the courtyard area there was a sweeping terracotta concrete slide and a large, shaded patio where some of the residents were performing the Easter season foot-washing ceremony. On the far side of the courtyard was a little brick structure that looked like a pagoda, and there was a multi-level dorm and a workshop in an adjoining courtyard. The inside and outside of the buildings were spotless.

When our time at *L'Arche* ended, we stepped beyond the gates of this oasis into seething streets, where men urinated at public urinals that were built into walls without any screens for modesty. Men also bathed in the street, but this time I didn't see women bathing, even though many Indian traditions concerning bathing are important to women. For example, a wife must bathe before entering her kitchen to prepare food for her family. I wondered how they managed to practice these traditions on the streets, where they cooked over coal fires.

I walked home with Father Ignatius while the rest of the group took the bus. Around us wafted strange but pleasant spicy smells. Merchant stalls sold garlands of marigolds to wear, eat, and use in worship services, along with strings of fragrant white flowers called *mogra* that were also worn and used in worship. As we threaded our way through narrow streets and alleyways, we passed displays of bumpy green bitter melons—a bit fatter than cucumbers—and very long green beans that I'd seen in Korean groceries in the United States. Food vendors were cooking on the street on great wok-like pans, while fruit vendors spread bananas in wheel configurations, with mangoes, grapes, and jackfruits so plentiful that they covered the merchants' stands and blankets.

All around was the faded grandeur of British colonial days. The neighborhoods' balconies were decorated with filigreed brickwork. The houses were set back in walled courtyards, which had become multiple-family dwellings. The buildings bore the mark of the gray-black filth that seems to have impregnated every building in the city, and over-population was apparent. Sometimes the vendors were double stacked, for behind the sidewalk stands stood small shops under corrugated roofs. Dogs wandered everywhere. I wondered where the cats were.

I know that the people of Kolkata have more pressing problems than to keep up colonial appearances; still, the buildings are a part of history and their ruin is a cultural loss. *The Hindustan Times* ran an article about the 1935 Currency Building, which the Archaeological Survey of India had declared a monument of national importance. Despite this protection, the building had fallen into disrepair. "Situated in one of the city's busiest areas, the building is virtually at the mercy of the elements. In fact, it has been converted to an open-air toilet by passers by." Blaming this on squabbles between the Archeological Society and factions that want to level the structure, the article goes on to say:

> ...though the beautiful interiors can be still glimpsed through half-open windows and gates, one realises that those interiors contain many invaluable objects that may no longer be fit to preserve...As the squabble continues, the grand structure, in ruins and overgrown with parasites, prepares for another monsoon...

In closing, the article warns that though the building is open to all, "It is safest to view it from the outside."[17]

The day ended at Maundy Thursday mass. Commemorating the Last Supper, which is the basis of communion, Maundy Thursday is my favorite ceremony of the Lutheran church year. Even though it is probably the saddest mass, its reminds us that Christ promised to be with us always. In that, it is very hopeful. I was looking forward to observing the ceremony with the Missionaries of Charity and wondered what the differences in service would be in their church.

When I arrived, the upper room of the Mother House was packed with worshippers. Some I recognized as volunteers; others were locals who were dressed in fine-looking saris. Although I couldn't participate in the Eucharist because I'm a Protestant, it was still an interesting and inspiring experience. As always, I enjoyed the sound of the nuns' voices when they sang and prayed. They have a distinctive accent: "th" is pronounced "d," "eh" is long "a," and while they shun the singsong rhythm of Indian dialects, it is reminiscent in their speech. Words are a little clipped and spoken with care, as if each word is separate, rather than rolled into the next as a sentence. Their sound is so consistent when they speak or sing as a group, it's if they are one voice.

Muslim prayers poured through the windows of the Mother House. The voices on the loudspeakers echoed and faded like circles of water in a pond that follow a splash. They blasted out over our service then dissipated into oblivion.

The room where mass was held was simple. The floors were smooth concrete covered by thin mats that offered no padding. Wooden benches lined the back walls for those who needed them, but most of the congregation was expected to sit on the floor. For this ceremony, the sisters had erected a special altar with candles and flowers. A large crucifix hung behind the main altar, and the altar was made from a table covered in cloth.

The liturgies of the Catholic and Lutheran services have similarities, but the symbols in the churches are different. As He hung on the cross at Mother Teresa's, Christ's knees were torn so badly that skin flaps drooped from the bloody wounds. Blood dripped from His pierced hands, feet, and sides. His head had fallen forward, His brow pierced by the crown of thorns. In this depiction of the crucifix lies a major difference between my church and the Catholic Church. The modern Lutheran Church characteristically displays a bare cross to symbolize that Christ came down from the cross and rose again from the dead. We emphasize the resurrection rather than the suffering. Another difference in service is the incense, which is not used in the Lutheran mass. Mary is yet another. She is honored as the mother of Christ in the Lutheran Church, but not venerated in the way she is by Catholics. In our little upper room at the Missionaries of Charity's House, where most masses were held, there were large statues of Jesus, robed and radiant. There were also statues of Mary, who is so important in the Missionaries of Charity's prayer lives and to all who pray the rosary, which is composed largely of Hail Marys.

All in all, the mass was a gentle experience that put me at peace about all I'd seen that day. It was fulfilling when I did not understand the mass to think my private thoughts and rest my mind in safe surroundings. And how could I not? There was beauty around me, along with people who cared about others. What better fuel for contemplation could there be after a day in the harsh realities of the world?

After mass I saw several sisters pile into an ambulance to go out into the city to find new patients. As I watched the last one climb in and the ambulance drive away, I knew I would miss them when I was home again.

SCOURING THE HALLS

On Friday morning I awoke at six fifteen. I hadn't even heard the Muslim prayers because I was tired from walking an hour and a half in the heat the day before, then kneeling at mass in the evening.

I had to rush to get ready and make it to the Mother House by seven. Fortunately, I'd developed a few shortcuts to make the morning easier. For example, I didn't put on makeup and I washed my hair at night then left it to dry naturally. Unfortunately, my hairdo had become quite wild and crazy-looking in the humidity—reminiscent of Albert Einstein.

Anyway, I hurried to the Mother House so as not to miss breakfast. The sisters encouraged volunteers to have breakfast at the Mother House after mass. Their food was safe, and breakfast was a time for camaraderie. It also served a safety function, because with everyone gathered in one place, the sisters could informally account for those who had registered as volunteers and find out whether anyone was ill or in need of help. If so, they would arrange medical care. If someone were missing for any period of time, the sisters would make an effort to find out if anything were wrong.

Breakfast at the Mother House was an opportunity to meet people, not only for friendship, but to walk with so that new people could find their way. It was also the time to speak with the sisters about concerns over activities or personality clashes taking place at the homes. The sisters preferred that volunteers discuss issues of conflict at the Mother House to keep negativity away from the missionary homes.

For breakfast, volunteers were served fat slabs of bread, sweet hot tea with milk, and the miniature bananas found in oriental groceries in the States. Sometimes there was enough bread to take two slices, but they were such huge chunks that two would have been too much for me, and I say this as a woman with a particularly healthy appetite. However, I hesitated to drink too much tea in the mornings, because the bathrooms at Kalighat included one seated toilette and one stall with those cement footprints over holes in the ground that are known as squatting pans. Since I feared catching intestinal parasites I was not ready to share the only seated toilet. I know you don't get parasites from the toilet seat; nevertheless, that was my irrational fear every time I sat down.

There was no toilet paper, but I carried "personal wipes" in a plastic bag for such situations. So far I had remained healthy, but a number of volunteers had dysentery. Also, Margaret, the eighteen-year-old volunteer from Singapore, had fallen ill. Her father, Dr. Fong, had returned to Singapore, so I'd been going by her room to check on her for the past couple of days. Margaret had been taking care of children in one of the *Shishu Bhavans* and had developed a cough and sore throat. I didn't like to see any volunteer develop a cough, because tuberculosis was rampant in our patient population, thus, I decided to monitor her illness. If she started coughing up blood or had night sweats with the cough, I'd have to make sure she called Dr. Fong. So far, her symptoms seemed more like a bad cold.

Respiratory infections and sore throat are the bane of anyone who is around small children. As every parent knows, disease spreads like wildfire through groups of young children, since they cough in each other's faces and wipe their runny noses with their hands, then share the germs with their parents and playmates as they touch everything and everyone they encounter. This is an example of why hand washing is so important in public health.

The importance of cleanliness in fighting disease and parasite transmission is one reason the Missionaries of Charity insist on scrubbing their homes so often; another is that it is a service that adds to the dignity of those for whom they care. But it is particularly difficult to keep adults with mental illness and their surroundings clean, and there were many such patients at *Kalighat*. Patients with severe mental illness defecate and urinate on the floor or wherever they sit, and there's nothing to do but clean it up. At *Kalighat*, as in every psych hospital on earth, they urinated and defecated where and when the spirit moved them. They removed their clothes and rocked back and forth, often wailing or talking to unseen companions. Sometimes medication helped; sometimes it did not. The sisters and volunteers got down on their hands and knees and scrubbed the floor several times a day, but still couldn't keep up with the incontinence that accompanies mental illness and serious disease. That is where the stone surfaces saved us. Aside from being easier to clean, they did not harbor odors as carpet would have.

At least a third of the women at *Kalighat* had some form of mental disability. Some of them had lived there for years and would never be sent home or to another facility. These women worked alongside *Kalighat* employees during the day, then lay down to sleep next to their fellow patients at night. They'd been beaten and discarded, probably abused all their lives. I couldn't imagine what had happened to them on the streets. Every time I thought I'd heard the worst story, something topped it the next day.

But the mental illness wasn't all trauma-induced; some of it was just old age. Chhaya had dementia. This was evident as she picked at her clothing, eyes darting about the room. Her fingers moved furtively over her gown, the characteristic aimless searching of dementia. She cried sporadically, but no tears came. The only time she did not cry was when she was cradled in someone's arms or eating—which she did with great enthusiasm.

Chhaya dragged herself to the bathroom, scooting along the smooth concrete floor on her bare bottom. As cruel as it sounds, this situation was not all bad. It allowed her some independence and helped her keep up her strength. Besides, as long as she chose to sit, she would not fall down, and keeping Chhaya from roaming in her demented condition would otherwise require restraints or pharmaceuticals that were not used at *Kalighat*. She was yet another reason the floors had to be clean.

It was Florence Nightingale who introduced strict standards of cleanliness to nursing. Her work to change the filthy environment of the British Army hospital at Sevastopol saved thousands during the Crimean War (1854-1856). When she returned to England, she learned that young peacetime soldiers died at nearly twice the rate of their civilian peers, and despite her success in the Crimea, she had to fight to institute cleanliness in peacetime military hospitals.

There are parallels between "Old Flo," as we called her behind our nursing professors' backs, and Mother Teresa. Florence Nightingale was a Unitarian, who at the age of seventeen felt a call from God to be a nurse. She said that "The connection between the health and the dwellings of the population is one of the most important that exists," and she, like Mother Teresa, passed on the legacy of providing the cleanest surroundings possible for those under their care.

Our days at *Kalighat* were full of cleansings. Water flew everywhere in the kitchen, from dishes, washing clothing by hand, cleaning medical instruments, and perpetually scrubbing the floors. Dishwashing was a production line performed by a team that moved dishes from one basin to another, each containing water and some containing soap. At the foot of the line stood the people with towels for drying.

Clothing and bedding were also washed in a progression of waters then hung out on the roof to dry in the spice-scented breeze. Only small people were allowed to go on the roof because there were weak spots and they feared a volunteer might plummet through. Inside or outside, clothing dries within an hour or two in Kolkata. That's one thing you could count on, despite humidity.

Aside from all the effort put into sanitizing everything by hand, other basic practices at *Kalighat* differed from those in the United States. In American hospitals and in homecare, we use disposable incontinence pads to keep patients clean and dry. At *Kalighat*, incontinent patients lie on rubber sheets, because everything must be washed by hand and laundry was already a never-ending task. The use of rubber sheeting is a long-standing tradition established by Mother Teresa for sanitary reasons, since disposable pads are costly, which seemed wasteful to her. Also, they are not available in many impoverished areas. From a nursing standpoint, those nonabsorbent rubber sheets posed a potential problem because patients' skin becomes wet from sweat and urine, increasing the chance that decubitus ulcers (pressure sores) will form.

I read that about 60,000 U.S. deaths result each year from pressure ulcers and the infections that follow. The cause of ulcer development is multifaceted, but I'm most familiar with them in the context of hospice. Dying patients are less mobile, and the weight of an immobile body compresses tissue under bony prominences, such as the tailbone and spine, inhibiting the blood supply to the compressed tissues. Blood carries the oxygen and nutrient supply throughout the body, and without it the skin dies and can fall away to a depth that exposes muscles and bone. Adding to this situation is that if disease has left the patient with poor ability to eat or inability to process food, the body does not have the building blocks it needs to repair damage. The bottom line is: Without good nutrition, skin does not heal.

Burned tissues, such as Kavita's, ulcerate quickly and may require another sort of cleansing—debridement. There are various debridement methods, but sharps debridement is a surgical procedure that involves cutting away dead tissue with a scalpel. After a serious burn, layers of skin die. The dead tissue tends to become blackened and is called necrotic. Necrotic tissue is no longer able to thrive, but it clings to the viable tissue. Necrotic tissue promotes infection and keeps the skin that is still capable of healing from getting oxygen and nutrients. For this reason, necrotic skin must be removed. When more gentle forms of debridement fail, sharps debridement may be the only way. It can be performed to remove necrotic tissue of any sort. For example, decubitus and diabetic ulcers may also warrant surgical debridement. One day I watched from a few cots over as they did this to Kavita's legs.

This was the first time I had gotten a good look at her wounds, because her legs were always bandaged. The gruesome sight reminded me of my first burn admission in the Johns Hopkins Regional Burn Center Intensive Care Unit. I was a nursing student working as a burn tech after school to get some ICU experience. When the patient was brought in, I could smell him all the way from the elevator, which was down the hall. At first I thought there was an electrical fire in the hospital.

They wheeled him in at a running pace and five of us surrounded the bed. The nurse who was handling the admission administered morphine, and a longtime nursing assistant wheeled a cart piled with instruments and supplies into the room. The nursing assistant had smelled the same smell now locked forever in my senses, but in her case, it sent her running for what we needed to treat the patient. She stood at the head of the bed and began to wash the man's charred head, while the rest of us were assigned to debride the body—literally pulling and scrubbing off damaged tissue.

I had seen this procedure once before I joined the burn team and had ended up puking my guts out into a biohazard bag. Let's just say that it is not a pleasant procedure. After that one false start, I never reacted so strongly again. I became proficient at burn care, and even as a nursing student I was able to carry out unpleasant burn care duties, such as full-body bandage changes—a physically and emotionally challenging task for nurse and patient.

While the Johns Hopkins Regional Burn Center ICU sounds like superb preparation for Kolkata, it was not. In fact, all it did was create more worries for me. In the US, ICU care is based upon high-tech precision monitoring. In Johns Hopkins ICUs, a nurse can expect to see a Swan-Ganz, which is a monitor that goes into the heart and can monitor everything from heartbeat to pressures. The sensor is placed in the right side of the heart, but looks left so that it can detect the most lethal form of heart failure while there is still time to reverse it. In fact, it detects nuances of changes, giving healthcare workers a fighting chance to treat deadly trends.

At Mother Teresa's we didn't have the means to detect life-threatening changes in the early stages. This is a problem, because burns, aside from being incredibly painful and deforming, are all about the cardiovascular and renal systems. The first priority is to monitor the patient's respiratory and cardiovascular functions. After all, without breath or a beating heart, the body will die. At *Kalighat*, I could take a pulse and listen to a chest, though the stethoscopes were woefully inadequate. The blood pressure cuffs were too large for the emaciated arms and wouldn't give a reading that I could trust.

There were so many other "must dos" in the United States that were irrelevant at *Kalighat*. In a Johns Hopkins ICU, I could get stat labs (meaning that the lab handled the specimen immediately and called the results to the nurses station, usually within an hour), which also helped detect subtle changes quickly. The Missionaries of Charity didn't have electric pumps whose computers precisely regulate the flow of IV fluids. Instead, we hung plastic bottles off poles as gravity drips and stuck hypodermic needles in the top of the plastic bottles to create ventilation. We regulated the dose by opening a lever and counting the number of drops per minute. There was no other choice in a place where the electricity may or may not work.

In an ICU, I would closely monitor for early signs of shock, which is where the body cannot maintain blood pressure and the vital organs don't receive enough blood. This is a continuous concern in burns. Since blood carries oxygen, and without oxygen, tissues—including those of the vital organs—die. The shock that occurs in the first few hours after a major burn likely results from neurological causes. However, burns continue to threaten shock as time passes, because fluid leaks from the wounds and out of the body, and because they damage blood vessels. Damage to the blood vessels may cause a massive fluid shift from the circulatory system into the tissues. The result is a life-threatening loss of blood pressure. But by the time you can see the patient's body beginning to swell from the fluid shift, it may be too late.

Loss of blood pressure sets off a cascade of events. For example, the heart pumps faster to try to keep the pressure stable—and it may succeed for a while. Nevertheless, multiple organs soon fail because the heart cannot sustain the frantic pace and the blood pressure inevitably drops. Once again, by the time you realize the blood pressure is dropping, it may be too late to save the patient.

Other facets of fluid balance are important factors in blood pressure. In American hospitals, we scrupulously measure how much fluid goes in and how much comes out as urine, which helps monitor kidney function and risk of shock, among other things. Optimal fluid regulation in burns is like Goldilocks' three bears choosing a bed—it can't be too much or too little; it must be just right. In the United States, we consider adequate fluid replacement over the first twenty-four hours to be of primary importance in burns, but Kavita did not receive immediate medical care. In fact, she had been injured for days before she was brought in, which put her in greater jeopardy.

I had more worries as I looked at Kavita. Burn injuries are insidious because life-threatening lung damage can develop over time. A burn victim can be breathing fine, then the throat suddenly swells shut or the lungs fill with liquid. They can die because of inhaled toxins from the smoke or because the lung tissues slough off and suffocate them. The lungs can also fill with fluid because the kidneys can't eliminate it, a reason for the obsession with measuring how much goes in and how much comes out. Unless the kidneys are getting rid of fluid, it is going into the tissues, not the circulatory system, and it is contributing to the threat, not the cure. Inhalation injury is deadly in the best ICUs, and we would not be able to do more than watch Kavita choke if it happened to her. However, the tissue on her face and upper body did not look burned—a classic tip-off that the lungs might be damaged—so perhaps her lungs were okay.

Infection is a frequent complication of burns, and I knew that Kavita had one without looking. I recognized the smell of *Pseudomonas*, a bacterium that has a characteristic odor and loves to live in the moist environment of wounds. In the burn units of the United States all procedures are sterile. I averaged ten to fifteen pairs of sterile gloves for a large-scale bandage change in the burn ICU. Since there is a high probability of infection in major burns, you have to change the gloves so you don't carry germs from one part of the body to another. At *Kalighat*, we were lucky to have enough gloves for nurses to change between patients, much less between wounds on the same patient. We often ended up washing our gloves as if they were our hands, but they soon became useless, as the water made them porous. Many times I just gave up, kept my hands as clean as possible, and didn't use gloves. Considering all this, I frankly found my hard-earned ICU training to be more hindrance than help under these conditions.

Pain from burns is severe. Most burn patients in the United States are fed enough morphine to put a horse down, and yet it controls their pain only enough to keep them from screaming. Having sustained a relatively small serious burn myself, I can tell you that the pain doesn't go away until the burn is healed. It is absolutely unrelenting.

At *Kalighat* they gave diazepam (the generic of Valium) for severe pain. The Indian doctor told me this was because he thought strong analgesics, such as morphine, would addict the patients. While a huge body of research disagrees with this opinion, I was bothered more by his assumptions than his ignorance of what causes addiction. With a scrunched-up nose and a sweep of his hand, he added that most of the patients had been addicts before they came in. If that were the case, I wonder why I never saw a case of withdrawal over the month that I was there. Alcohol and drug withdrawal would begin within 24 hours of the last fix.

Diazepam has no analgesic effect, except to relax muscle spasms, but does calm the patients and often makes them sleep, so it's better than nothing. I kept my mouth shut about the highly addictive qualities of benzodiazepines—the drug family diazepam belongs to—fearing he'd ban that too.

From a practical standpoint, however, if the Missionaries of Charity had narcotics in the house, it would be a sure invitation to robbers. They already couldn't stock the supply cabinets with a lot of extras because the ambulance drivers stole things.

Other than Kavita, I didn't see anyone in obvious major pain. I attribute this to the placebo effect: when patients trust in their care and believe they will get better, they do. It's been clinically proven that physiological changes occur when people believe a treatment will make them better, and the patients at *Kalighat* certainly believed they were getting superior treatment. Trust and kindness abounded at *Kalighat*, soothing and healing in ways that the medical community in the United States seems not to fathom in the midst of our technological advances.

The pain management issue was one I struggled with at home as well as in India. Dame Cecily Saunders and the hospice movement she founded have greatly influenced the way the Western medical establishment is beginning to regard pain management. Still, a lot of work remains to be done in this field. In the United States, only three percent of medical schools have a required course on pain management, according to a 2003 Association of American Medical Colleges (AAMC) survey of 125 medical schools.[18] One result is that the patient gets blamed when the doctor cannot identify a physiological source for the pain. In fact, most chronic pain patients have a condition that can't be identified on x-rays, so imagine my surprise when I heard Johns Hopkins nursing students, who were working a rotation in the chronic pain clinic discussing a patient. "There's nothing wrong with that woman," one said. "Yeah, she's just going to have to get over herself," the other responded. A chronic pain patient myself, I cringed. My x-rays aren't impressive either; but believe me, the pain is there.

It's sad but true; studies have shown that U. S. medical people—including nurses—judge other people's pain harshly and probably unfairly. We count on facial expressions and changes in vital signs, rather than the patient's word, to gauge what's going on in the patient's own body. Those signs may work in a gunshot wound or just post-surgery, but the default for the body is to normalize what it can. Because of this, all those signs may be masked in a chronic pain patient who has simply learned to carry on daily life in pain.

Those who study pain know that there are various types, such as bone, visceral, spasm, nerve, and soft tissue. Different types of medicines and pain-management strategies work better for each type of pain. Narcotics are not the drugs of choice in all severe pain. For example, anticonvulsants and certain antidepressants may alleviate nerve pain, and non-steroidal anti-inflammatories, such as ibuprofen and aspirin, work on bone pain. While we use strong analgesics in hospice work, we also use methods other than pharmaceuticals. Techniques such as massage and therapeutic touch are proven to relieve pain in some situations. I personally have had great success with chiropractic care for cranial, neck, and shoulder pain. Of course, any therapy choice must weigh potential side effects against the need for medication, because it's always a trade-off. The rule of thumb is to use what will allow the patient the best quality of life as defined by the patient.

Pain is not just a physiological response. There is a psychological component as well, and that doesn't mean that pain is imagined. Two phenomena illustrate that pain is not just a stimulus and response: (I) Phantom limb pain, which the patient perceives in appendages that are no longer attached, and (2) The soldier who is injured on the battlefield, yet feels no pain until a later time. While phantom limb pain is excruciating and difficult to quell, it occurs without a stimulus because the limb that hurts is no longer there. For example, a man who has had an above-the-knee amputation of the leg may feel pain in the toes of the amputated limb. The flip side of this is battlefield injuries, which obviously occur with painful stimuli—stepping on a landmine, being shot or bayoneted—yet the victim may or may not feel pain at the time of injury and will continue to fight or pull a buddy to safety.[19]

It has even been shown that people "feel" each other's pain. Researchers have conducted brain scans of persons observing a loved one receiving slight electrical shocks and found that the experience activates a region of the brain involved in processing pain. The same area showed activity when the subjects themselves received electrical shocks. "As people watched their companions suffer, their brains appeared to recreate the unpleasant experience, in effect allowing them to feel their partners' pain."[20]

So all of this is to say that love, compassion, and human touch do ease suffering. Patients at *Kalighat* were safe and respected. It gave them the resolve to heal and to live. In the end, I prefer the option of strong painkillers in the medical setting, but touch does marvelous things, as I learned when I held comatose patients' hands in the cardiac ICU and watched dangerously erratic heartbeats calm. Perhaps there's no explaining the effect of touch and caring physiologically, but one should never discount their power either.

CEASELESS CRIES FOR HELP

Today was another race against time. I started at seven in the morning with mass and breakfast at the Mother House, worked two shifts at *Kalighat,* and finally sat down in the restaurant at seven-thirty at night. I was filthy, and my face burned from the pollution, sweat, who knows what.

I awakened at five o'clock a.m., concerned about Mustafa, a man with blisters I suspected were varicella (chicken pox). The thought crossed my mind that I might not recognize smallpox if I saw it, and India is a land that totters at the edge of war with Pakistan. There have already been nuclear threats, and the possibility of chemical and biological weapons comes with this territory. The use of smallpox in a biological attack is one of the most feared among healthcare workers. I had the vaccine, but that was decades ago, and I wasn't sure it was still effective.

After a tight moment, I reasoned that a biological attack would mean an epidemic, not an isolated case, and my worries subsided. While varicella seemed most likely, I ran through symptoms of other diseases in my head. In infectious disease it is important to consider the differential diagnosis (other possibilities).

Mustafa had a few blisters on his face, arms, and legs, but his trunk was crowded with them. The blisters seemed to be filled with a clear, watery-looking substance, and they were small—a little-finger tip or less in circumference—and fairly round in appearance. Some of them had burst and scabs were forming. I hadn't seen varicella since my children had it in the 1970s, and such diseases often look different on dark skin, because redness doesn't show as well. Most children survive this disease, but child-hood diseases are always worse in adults, and Mustafa was a very sick man who looked skeletal to begin with. Also, some other disease brought him into *Kalighat*, and I didn't know what it was.

Yesterday afternoon, he had looked feverish and dazed, though we'd been trying to lower his temperature by keeping him cool. It was an uphill battle. He'd stopped eating days before, and now he was breathing at a rate of forty-four breaths per minute, which is way too fast and a sign of how much his body was struggling. All I could do was try to lower his tempera-ture so that he would be more comfortable.

No sooner had I turned from him than another man was brought in as an emergency. He lay on his cot and stared at the ceiling until I ap-proached him. As I stood over the cot, there was a flicker of expression in his eyes, as if he detected my presence, but other than that, there was no response. I turned him over and saw scars on his back that looked like he had been whipped. Light pink tissue appeared where the dark had been ripped away. No one knew the man, so there was no explanation as to why or how this had happened.

On the female side, there was a woman with seven three-centime-ter-long keloids (raised scars) progressing up her left forearm. I was told that self-mutilation was not unusual among the women of *Kalighat*. In the United States, we most often see self-mutilation in psychotics and people with Borderline Personality Disorder, either of which can be brought on by biological factors or a life of abuse.

There were also victims of less intentional situations, such as Deep-ika, who looked like she had the thalidomide birth defect syndrome. In the 1950s and 60s, thalidomide was given to pregnant women for nausea and insomnia. The symptoms that made me think Deepika had the tha-lidomide syndrome were that her legs were flippers, and her arms were abbreviated, with the ulnas—the bones on the little-finger side of the fore-arm—curved and turned up, similar to the bowl of a spoon. Her head was the only feature of normal size. She was in her twenties, with very dark skin, big brown eyes, and a long chin.

While rarely used in the United States these days, thalidomide re-mains a valid part of treatment in leprosy, specifically in moderate to severe cases of *erythema nodosum leprosum* (ENL). For that reason, it is still used in India.

Later that morning, I walked by Deepika's cot. She held up her left index finger and made a face that said, "it hurts." As I examined the finger, I could see a severely swollen infected area around one side of the cuticle. I had to get rid of the pus to release the pressure that was causing such pain, so I gathered the equipment to lance it. I also picked out an oral antibiotic to help prevent the infection from spreading to her bone.

Deepika cried like a child when I lanced the infected area and squeezed out the pus. She wouldn't look at me when I applied the bandage, and I felt terrible, but I'd done what I had to do. Oddly, I knew what to do because I bite my nails. When I was a child, I suffered a similar infection. My father, who was a physician, took me into the hospital, where they lanced the infection and explored to assure it had not spread to the bone.

I came back for the afternoon shift to give the injections. Volunteers were generally scarce in the afternoon because of the evening prayers at the Mother House. Normally, the novices gave medications in the afternoon, but during the Easter season they had to attend prayers. I couldn't begrudge them the afternoon off for extra prayers at Easter, because the day-to-day schedule they keep is extremely demanding. The sisters start their day at four-forty in the morning, get fifteen minutes for breakfast, forty minutes for each lunch and dinner, about an hour for rest and free time, and the remainder of the time before lights-out at ten at night is for work and prayer. They spend most of their day on their knees, either working or praying.

The injectable medications at *Kalighat* were in glass ampoules, which I utterly despise. I'm not sure why medications are still packaged in them, because healthcare workers get cut opening them, which is exactly what happened to me that afternoon. I'd been told to whack the ampoules at the slender neck with a file and not to attempt to file around the edge and break off the top as I had been taught in nursing school, because these particular ampoules would come apart in my hand. I, however, was stubborn and had to follow my Western ways, so I worked for the rest of the afternoon with an open wound where the jagged edges of an ampoule had sliced the side of my right index finger around the knuckle.

Aside from that, the afternoon shift began with an extra dose of chaos: Someone on the last shift had walked off with the only keys to the medicine cabinets. We didn't know who had them or whom to contact to get them back. And, of course, there were no extra keys.

Before running off to mass, one of the sisters jimmied the medicine cabinets like a pro so I could give injections, but the bandages and anti-septics remained locked. In a dire emergency, I figured I could put my FBI lock-picking skills into action, but that career was an explanation I preferred not to make to everyone. At *Kalighat*, I was a nurse.

As the sisters were leaving, another worry arose: no other volunteers had arrived. My mouth must have been hanging open as Sister Georgina told me to trust in God, then disappeared out the door, leaving me with almost a hundred patients. But soon the volunteers trickled in. Though none were nurses, they passed out pills and cared for patients while I gave the injections. Oh, for the days I complained of having five patients. One to one hundred is not a good nurse-to-patient ratio.

I was so glad I had written the patients' medication orders in my personal notebook, since the medicine administration books remained secured in a padlocked desk. The worst of it for the volunteers was that there were no gloves for the shift, because they were locked somewhere upstairs in a storage area I didn't have access to. This is a significant risk in a facility where there is leprosy and scabies, not to mention purulent wound drainage.

Before getting involved in routine medication administration, I walked around the wards to triage emergencies. On one bed lay a woman who had been very chatty until that morning, when she had been almost non-responsive. While I could find no apparent cause, I feared she had begun the process of dying. No vast physiological changes had been evident in the morning, but her distance from what was going on around her was profound, and I had a feeling that something had changed—or, as we say in medicine, there had been "an event."

When I went to her cot to see how she was doing, one look told me she was dead. She was on her side with eyes fixed and staring toward the wall, and her skin had blanched. I didn't need to touch pulse points to confirm what I saw.

I sat on her cot and laid my hand on her arm. Her body was cold. I started to turn her to listen to her heart and pronounce her death according to the guidelines for hospice nurses in the United States. It was then that I realized she had bled out. Gastric bleeds do not merely shed a few drops of blood; in the worst case they gush the body's entire blood supply from the mouth and/or rectum within a couple of minutes. When that happens, there is so much bleeding that it can spill off from the bed and onto the floor. This woman's bleed had been a bit gentler, but it was all over the cot beneath her body, and sure enough, I was sitting in it.

Without gloves or knowing her full diagnosis, I decided to go through the motions of pronouncing death. I had no doubt she was dead, I'm just a stickler for the rules, so I listened to her heart for a few minutes as she lay on her side. With gloves, I would have done her the courtesy of washing her and changing her clothing, but the best I could do in this case was tidy her bed and leave her in peace until someone from the mortuary came.

I gathered the volunteers who were caring for the patients in the female ward and informed them of the death, as well as the reason we would not be honoring her by washing her body. I ordered them not to risk their health by handling blood and other body fluids without gloves, then accompanied those who wanted to say goodbye to this dear woman. Unfortunately, there were no interpreters to help me talk to the patients in surrounding cots and answer their questions. All I could do was motion to them that the woman was at peace.

With volunteers gathered around, I sat down next to her again and put my hand on her arm. I showed them the blood, answered their questions, and then left them to say their goodbyes. Up to the point when the undertakers approached the cot, I noticed volunteers sitting near her and taking time to talk as best they could to the women on the nearby cots. It was nice to see their respect for people whom they would never have encountered outside this confounding city. It was a death I will never forget, but I will also remember that she was happy at *Kalighat*, that she had friends and wore a smile on her face every time I saw her until that last time.

But the shift had just begun and I had to turn to other patients. Caring for a woman, whom I'll call Anuradha, made the shift worth going through. She was in her early twenties with loosely waved black hair that fell to her shoulders, which meant she had not come in with lice or her head would have been shaved. She was slender, but not emaciated, and seemed to have good muscle tone, so I thought she had not been lying in bed long.

We didn't speak a common language, but she pointed to her swollen belly, opening and closing her fist. Her black eyes pleaded for help. I tried pantomiming cuddling a baby because she looked pregnant enough to deliver at any moment, but she waved her hand and shook her head emphatically "no." My next thought was that she might be having bladder spasms, which happens with obstructions because the bladder tries to force out the excess of urine. When I examined her abdomen, I could feel her bladder at the umbilicus, so I decided to insert a catheter. This time there was no one around to consult about the catheterization, which was good, considering the lesson I'd learned with Kavita.

As soon as I got the catheter in, the urine gushed out. I drained off more than two liters before the output began to slow. When I came back later, another liter had drained. This poor woman's bladder must have been on the verge of a rupture. By way of comparison, the average renal system processes about eighteen hundred cubic centimeters (ccs) in twenty-four hours, which is one and eight-tenths liters. When I left after three hours, Anuradha was smiling again and looking much more comfortable. It was a small victory, but it made a difference to me, and I clung to it.

The non-functioning bladder was not her only problem: Several months before, she had experienced what sounded to me like sciatic nerve pain, beginning in the lower back around the inner aspect of the pelvic bone, then shooting down the back of her leg. Now Anuradha had no sensation in her legs, and her fingers were becoming numb. Her feet were swollen well beyond what might be expected from a woman's menstrual cycle or any other non-pathological explanation I could think of. She had been sent out for an X-ray to see whether she had a tumor or spinal injury of some sort. More tests and imagery, such as a CAT scan, would have helped with diagnosing her, but the Indian doctor would have to order that, and he only came a couple of times a week.

My greatest fear was that this woman had ALS, also known as Lou Gehrig's disease. Amyotrophic lateral sclerosis is a degenerative nerve disease that causes the patient to progressively lose the use of all muscles. Eventually, even the muscles that control breathing cease to work and that's how the patient dies. The result isn't sudden respiratory arrest—the ability to breathe slips slowly away, and it's a horrible thing to go through. Part of the hell of this disease is that the patient does not lose mental function and doesn't know what physical ability he or she will lose next. There is no known cure.

While it is hard to select a "bravest" patient that I've seen in my time at hospice, one ALS patient stands out. Her name was Lynn, and Anuradha reminded me of her. Lynn was also in her twenties and had lost many functions by the time I met her. She couldn't voluntarily move her body, except that she could swallow pureed foods and move her eyelids, as well as the big toe of one foot. Her family had rigged up a board that she could press with the toe and ring a bell when she needed attention.

She was staying in the hospice for respite care while the family took a vacation, and we pumped liquefied food into her mouth through needleless sixty cc syringes. That was the only way she could eat. Basically, this pretty young woman, with thick blonde hair and deep brown eyes, could blink, swallow, and move her big toe. That was her life. She, like Anuradha, was one of those patients who tore at my heart.

One day, we were changing Lynn's bed, which entailed rolling her from side to side to get the sheets on and off without getting her out of bed. We got the sheets changed without problems, then set about positioning pillows under her arms and legs to avoid pain and pressure ulcers. Every time we moved her, she rang that bell. My coworker and I placed and moved pillows, changed her position from side to side, and asked her a hundred questions, to which she responded by blinking once for yes and twice for no. Throughout the process the bells continued, and we became more frustrated over how to make her feel better.

At last, my coworker leaned her elbows on the bed railing and said, "Dear, I have no idea what you want."

Two bells answered, then one more. My heart sank. I was out of ideas. My coworker's face reflected a sudden flash of suspicion. She looked at me, then back to the patient. "Are you screwing with us?" she asked gingerly, and the bell went off like a fire alarm.

The patient smiled and we burst into laughter. How on earth a woman at that stage of disease could even dream of playing a joke is beyond me.

She never went home from that respite visit. She died to the world just a few days later. I say died to the world because she lives in me.

Anuradha, too, died to the world. She was sent out to a hospital where she developed severe bedsores. Infections ensued that went systemic, and, too late, she returned to the sisters in August to spend her last days.

Of all the seriously ill patients I've cared for as a nurse or volunteer, Anuradha makes me the saddest. Life never gave her a chance. She was born poor in India, which is profoundly impoverished, and aside from being female, she was probably a *Dalit*, a member of the untouchable class, whom the upper classes believe contaminate the air that decent people breathe. These are not issues I've had to deal with, and hers were not troubles I could truly say I understand.

The sisters had sent her to the hospital hoping that doctors could solve the mystery of her paralysis and enable her to go home, where her son waited. Unfortunately, the hospital stay did not resolve the source of the paralysis and lying in a hospital bed caused the condition that was to be her demise. She returned to the sisters' care when she was beyond hope. Stricken with TB and AIDS, her bedsores were to the bone and her immune system was not able to fight off the infection.

Anuradha would never go home to her four-year-old son, and I would hear about her bedsores and death in an email from Carolyn as I sat in my living room all safe and sound. I am at least twice Anuradha's age. It doesn't seem fair.

AN UNEXPECTED DAY OFF

Trouble came from an unexpected source—my feet, which were raw and swollen. Part of the problem was that they were constantly wet due to sweat and the perpetual washing of floors. In the kitchen they threw water across the walking surfaces several times a day, and everyone got drenched. We never dried out in that place, so it was easy for fungus to grow. On top of that, I'd developed an addiction to fresh lime, salt, and soda water drinks, and my feet swelled from the excess salt. Plus, my sandals had rather abrasive inner soles. It wasn't bothersome when my feet were healthy, but it felt like sandpaper on the macerated skin. So, I decided to take a day off for rest and reflection, and also to buy some different sandals.

I'd awakened from a dream about *Kalighat*—I'd been trying to figure a way to organize the workflow more efficiently. One major problem was the organization of medical supplies. Medications from all over the world were thrown into boxes, and everyone wondered what to do with them because drugs didn't have the same name from country to country. For example, people raised outside the United States knew acetaminophen (Tylenol) as paracetamol, yet I had never heard of it. While I continued to struggle with the names of medications, I was gradually picking up terminology from the other nurses. What I wanted to do was devise a translation chart for all those who would follow me, but that would take more linguistic knowledge than I had.

Lying on my bed, I put my feet up on pillows, hoping to relieve some of the puffiness, and began to scribble notes. I had wanted to capture so many memories on paper—the grit of a day in Kolkata on my skin; the sensation of being drenched in sweat but not feeling overheated; people stretched out on blankets on the sidewalks at night and in the morning; and the colonies of people who lived along the walkways under shelters made of black plastic sheeting. It wasn't like I would have imagined. For example, the people who slept on the streets didn't curl up next to the buildings or hug the curb. They stretched out in the middle of the sidewalks, sometimes crosswise. They cooked on the sidewalk in pots of fire fueled by coal, which, in combination with the enormous number of automobiles burning what smelled like diesel fuel, accounted for at least some of the blackness that shrouded the buildings.

Near a bus stop that I passed every day was a vendor who had hung a rope from the canopy that shielded his stand from the blazing sun. One end of this rope was aflame and people used it to light their cigarettes. The combination of Kolkata's pollution and cigarette smoking must be particularly lethal to the respiratory system.

Since I wasn't going in to work, I ate breakfast in the hotel. The Mother House and *Kalighat* were the only places where I'd eaten since leaving the Oberoi, because the food in Kolkata could be dangerous. A few of the volunteers had been hospitalized, but the people in my hotel had avoided diarrhea and hepatitis A, which were both among the diseases spread through water and food here. A typical headline in the *Times of India* read: "Spurt in gastro cases, hundreds in hospital." When asked about the disease that was spreading throughout the city, Pravakar Chatterjee, director of health services, remarked: "I have heard that some people have been admitted to the hospital. There is no suggestion of an outbreak at the moment." Another official claimed, "Most cases are slum dwellers and do not follow proper hygienic measures."[21] I'm afraid there were just too many cases in far-flung sectors of Kolkata for me to buy that explanation.

During breakfast, my own digestive system grabbed my attention, and I ventured into the restaurant's ladies room for the first time. I was displeased to find a squatting pan, though this one was a porcelain product with a flush and toilet paper. Despite the relative luxury compared to the squatting pans at *Kalighat*, I still had to fill a bucket with water to push fecal matter to the back of the pan, where there was a hole that things washed into to be flushed. The pans were a little longer than two, maybe two and a half feet long, by one and a half feet across. They allowed for a position that was useful for expelling waste from the body but required quite the balancing act for one who wasn't used to them. In addition, it was important to make sure clothing was securely tucked about the body before squatting. I definitely didn't want my trouser legs dragging through that muck.

While I, like most Westerners, complained to myself about bathroom facilities and lack of gloves at *Kalighat*, there was actually an advantage for me being in conditions that heightened my awareness of sanitation issues: it discouraged me from biting my nails. So while I had not been losing weight, at least I was kicking one lifelong bad habit.

After breakfast, I went out to look for shoes and a fingernail brush. However, the morning shopping venture proved unsuccessful. As it turned out, the shops didn't open until "after ten," and I'd learned that "after ten" meant at some point after ten, perhaps an hour, perhaps more. One morning at the Oberoi, I was told to come back "after eleven o'clock" to exchange cash. After eleven, I was told to come back "in an hour or so." This lack of care for exact time is typical throughout India. In the restaurant, the waiter inevitably put the butter on the table toward the end of the meal, after the bread had been eaten. Buses came when they came; there was no schedule. You just had to go out on the street and wait. You could go out at the same time each day and wait an hour or ten minutes. One of the nurses missed her flight to Australia because the plane left two hours early. And fight though I did to keep my American expectations of precision timing, it was a useless endeavor, so I decided to go back to my room for a couple of hours and keep my feet up.

So far on this trip, shopping had been intimidating at best. Street vendors overwhelmed me, as did the young children who begged. The beggar children latched onto my arms, and I ended up dragging them along with me because they would not let go. Giving alms drew crowds, so it was a big mistake to do so. It was like a grotesque carnival.

Later in the afternoon I ventured back to New Market, but this time I took my secret weapons: Phillis and Margaret. With them at the lead, my shopping trip was a pleasure. Nonetheless, in Kolkata, getting there is always an adventure and today, I took my first ride in a rickshaw.

Outside my hotel there were always lines of black rickshaws with red and gold-painted trim, but without my friends I would have never tried my luck in one. To my surprise, it was largely a pleasant experience, except that I felt terrible about having a tiny man haul me over the crater-ridden streets and across tram tracks. Sitting in a rickshaw, I was high above the crowd and felt a bit like a stereotype of a rich colonial. I didn't like the image. Still, the man made his living pulling a rickshaw, and he needed my business. I paid what he asked without haggling and gave him a nice tip, which I hoped would allow him to knock off a little early.

The rickshaw ride took us through tiny alleys lined with homes and shops. The foods of the street vendors were artfully displayed, especially the fruits and fruit drinks. Pastries looked intriguing: conical fried items, twists, spheres, and curlicues. But with the gastroenteric epidemic and the number of volunteers who had been hospitalized, I wasn't keen on trying my luck. Besides, the food at the Circular was better than the Oberoi Grand's, in my opinion, and at a fraction of the price. I had no desire to go elsewhere. But even at the Circular I could feel grit on the outside of drink bottles. It was not their fault, however. The bottles were transported in open trucks, and the water that they might be rinsed in was likely to deposit bacteria that are worse than the dirt. Using a straw was the best solution.

The New Market sells everything imaginable: lots of teas and spices, chickens and lambs, and a huge array of fabrics, clothing, and accessories. I had one unpleasant surprise in the area that housed the livestock: people have the animals slaughtered while they wait.

Everywhere were cheap trinkets, plastic bangles, rubber shoes, and feather dusters; but there were also rich-looking, hand-beaded textiles that I would have snapped up if they would have fit into my suitcase. My husband had said in an email that he hadn't received any letters from me. I had mailed them a couple of weeks before, so I knew the mail wasn't reliable and I was not about to mail anything expensive. Other volunteers had confirmed that they'd mailed packages that never arrived at their destinations. I'd even heard that people at the post office sometimes steal the stamps off the letters, so I resolved to buy only what I could hand-carry back home.

New Market had some disturbing aspects. It was a veritable crush of humanity, and men followed me around hoping to force me into shops where they would collect a commission. In the shops, salesmen hurled themselves at me with no concept of Western psychological needs for maintaining distance. While they stood entirely too close for my comfort, they did not touch, and they were infuriated if anyone reached out to touch them. It was worth the ire sometimes, however, because nothing I said made them back off.

Even if I wanted to buy something, I had to bargain, which I didn't like. It left me feeling stupid and used. Phillis, on the other hand, was a killer negotiator. We never paid anywhere near what was asked. For instance, when we looked at silks, the asking price was one thousand five hundred rupees. We paid six hundred fifty rupees after she got through with them. The asking price for silk pashminas was six hundred fifty rupees. We paid four hundred rupees—less than ten U.S. dollars.

Phillis started out by asking, "What is your best price?" They said, "One thousand five hundred rupees," to which she responded, "Six hundred." Haggling ensued until we walked out, saying we didn't have that kind of money. The shop men followed us out into the corridor, negotiating all the way.

Phillis just kept saying, "Six hundred." When we reached the alley, the owner said in mock desperation, "Can't you come up a little?" Phillis said, "Six hundred fifty," and back we went with the proprietor talking a mile a minute.

In the end, I bought four silks and she bought several, but I didn't see how many because I went to look at pashminas. I got my best price for the pashminas, and they knocked off two hundred rupees per piece when Phillis stepped up to the counter to help me bargain.

One delightful moment came when I walked into a pharmacy, and the woman behind the counter immediately crossed herself when she saw my Miraculous Medal. It reinforced what a great impact Mother Teresa has had upon these people. Her picture was everywhere. I even saw a poster of her in a cinema near New Market. Film in India is a popular form of entertainment, with Bollywood—the Indian version of Hollywood—pushing out an average of more than one thousand films per year. While these films are mostly formulaic, lighthearted song-and-dance films that depict wealth and romance in extremely colorful settings, they draw avid fans. Mother Teresa's poster got equal billing.

At the pharmacy I bought some low-dose furosemide, a diuretic for my swollen feet. I was sure that the walk and cutting out my beloved lime and salt sodas would help too. After all, the hot season had begun in earnest, I was drinking tons of water, and the humidity ensured that I stayed wringing wet all day long. I drank tea instead of coffee, though tea has just as many diuretic properties, and I didn't even consider having alcohol. As much as I enjoy wine with dinner at home, it had never occurred to me to try it in Kolkata. It was probably the dehydration factor that made it unappealing—that and the fear of being drugged.

As the onslaught of humanity and the aggression of the beggars became more familiar, I was more at ease on the streets. Even the buses, which tended to be packed, had their charm. And when I say they were packed, I mean beyond standing room only. Eventually, I learned to hang off the side, as was the custom. How I became oblivious to the safety issues hanging off a bus in India presented, I'll never know. I read about one bus that was running between cities and plunged into a ditch when it tried to overtake a motorcycle. Twelve passengers were killed and eighty-five injured, many of whom were sitting on top of the bus.

With all those bodies crowded together in hundred-degree heat and no air conditioning, you'd think the smell of sweat would overpower you, but the people smelled nothing like that. Perhaps my body smelled the same, so I no longer sensed others. I don't know, but I'd been nose to pit with many as we suspended our arms from the overhead rails to stay upright as the buses bobbed and weaved in and out of traffic, honking like madmen all the way.

The buses had shrines in the front, which was understandable considering the traffic. Most had Hindu images, such as the ubiquitous blue Krishnas, but many featured several religions side by side—including images of Mother Teresa paired with Christ and Mary. Buses were ornately decorated on the inside with squiggly painted decorations along the ceilings. There were often garlands of *mogra*, a sweet-scented white flower with bell-shaped blooms, hanging near the shrines at the front of the buses.

Accompanying the rides through the city were a cacophony of sounds and an assault on the olfactory senses. Phillis said that the honking stems from the tradition of riding bicycles, when people rang the bell as they approached someone or went around a corner. This made sense to me, but why they didn't honk was baffling. The other day I was hit by a car yet again. The driver gave no warning, but fortunately he had just turned a corner and hadn't had time to build up a full head of steam before veering into the crowd. While it was only a little bump, I was infuriated. I slammed both fists down onto the car as soon as I felt it hit me and didn't even think about what I was doing. The driver turned around looking quite terrified but didn't stop or roll down a window to ask whether I was hurt.

I've heard that when cars hit pedestrians in Kolkata, crowds sometimes torch the car with the driver in it. Considering that he had been well into the crowd of pedestrians, I hoped that this thought crossed his mind and that he stopped using his car to make people get out of the way.

Vehicles have left their mark on Kolkata's way of life, and affect the sensory experience, since they exude vile puffs of diesel fuel. The smells around Kolkata were a mixture of bad and good. In some places, the street gutters smelled of urine and feces, mixed with the smell of outdoor cooking on coal. Still, the overall impression was more of sumptuous foods and spices.

On the route to *Kalighat*, we passed a number of curious sights. One of them always disturbed me: a fetid pond where people bathed. I didn't know what was in it, but the surface seemed slimy and bubbly, and debris had been cast into it. Numbered piers stretched into the water that looked almost like swimming starting blocks. I shuddered at the thought of a swim team working out in there.

As for my daily routines, I had perfected a method for running the obstacle course of men who worked, slept, and bathed on the sidewalks between the Circular Hotel and the Mother House. I wore baggy clothes that covered everything but my head, hands, and feet, and I never met their eyes. I charged ahead with my swift East Coast-U.S. walk, as if I were hurrying to an important meeting. When the sidewalk was too crowded, which would have forced me close to strange men, I walked in the street, preferring to take my chances with the traffic. But one afternoon I couldn't get near the Mother House because Muslims were lining the sidewalk and street for prayer at an adjacent mosque. They were actually kneeling in the street amidst the traffic, an extreme expression of faith.

Incidentally, I at last mastered the art of readjusting when the Kolkata transportation system provided unexpected stress. Recently, I took a different bus than I usually do, because I was told it stopped near my hotel. The bus driver told me to disembark at a stop I didn't recognize, but he insisted that it was the closest place to the Circular where the bus would stop.

As I stepped off, he pointed the way for me to go, and—like a ninny—I obeyed. I walked to a circle, where I met some Japanese volunteers who spoke a little English. They recognized me and motioned for me to follow them. They were giggling and I feared some of my adventures in public transportation stories had become such bestsellers among the English-speaking volunteers, that they were now available in translation to anyone who needed a good laugh.

Anyway, off I went with them, but after a block or so, one of them asked whether I was trying to get to the Mother House. As it turns out, they had assumed I was staying in a hotel on Sudder Street near theirs and hadn't realized I was headed for a hotel near the Mother House. And so began the odyssey of being hopelessly lost as I set off on a trek down alley-like streets in the Muslim section. I was the only woman without a veil, and the leering eyes made that painfully clear.

Nonetheless, I recovered fairly quickly. I found a reputable-looking hotel, asked for directions, and tipped the doorman to find a cab. He negotiated a price for me before I got in, so the cabby knew he would be blacklisted from the hotel's clientele if he cheated me. I arrived at my hotel without incident, for a change. I was finally getting the hang of it.

EMERGENCIES

This morning a TB patient in respiratory crisis was admitted. Volunteers had found him in the street near the Howrah train station, unable to walk. As he crouched on his elbows and knees on the cot, his emaciated arms formed the classic respiratory distress tripod, which uses gravity to relieve the chest of body weight and allows the lungs to expand more easily. He was delirious and panting and didn't look like he was going to make it through the night, so I gave him something to calm him and dry up the mucus. My gut feeling was, however, that he was beyond help.

This man, I was informed, was a regular who would not take his medications when he was released. His left lung fields emitted a snoring sound and there were wheezes in the lower right lobe. The snoring sounds are called rhonchi. Rhonchi indicated liquid in the lungs, while the high-pitched wheezes indicated obstruction. These were not good findings.

He appeared to be in his forties to fifties, but I'd learned that appearances could be deceptive in this harsh environment. He was cachectic, which means he'd lost virtually all body fat and his muscles were wasted as well. The emaciation is consistent with TB, but he didn't have a fever, and I didn't know enough about tuberculosis to decide what the lack of fever meant. I wasn't sure whether I was seeing advanced TB, TB and AIDS, AIDS with pneumonia, complicated bronchitis with starvation, lung cancer, or any number of other maladies. And, there was no lab or x-ray to help me eliminate diagnoses. So many times at *Kalighat* I felt inadequate. This was one of them.

The day was not shaping up well. I had two other patients near death. One was a woman I'll call Izmat, who was a potential bleed-out. Izmat appeared to be in her late forties, and until today had been energetic with a quick smile and easy laugh. She was one of Australian nurse Carolyn Milton's favorites and had been fine yesterday, but had become minimally responsive over the morning shift. One of the sisters told me that last night Izmat had had seizures and had vomited blood. They gave her the muscle relaxant diazepam to ease the seizures, but by morning she was lethargic and would not open her eyes or respond when spoken to or shaken. She did open her eyes for a few seconds when I washed her face.

Like the TB patient, Izmat had fluid bubbling in the left lung fields, probably from aspirating blood or vomit, but possibly from bleeding respiratory system tissues. She was breathing at about thirty breaths per minute; the norm is twelve to twenty. If she continued breathing at that rate—or if it were to increase, which was not unlikely considering the state of her health—she might end up with more carbon dioxide than oxygen in her system. Among other bad outcomes, this can lead to death.

Her carotid arteries were bounding at ninety-four beats per minute, and beating with such force that I didn't have to touch her to count. I could just look at her neck. This meant her heart was working awfully hard. The pulses in her feet, however, were faint and her abdomen soft. The main significance of the soft abdomen in her case was that I didn't feel swelling from a gastric bleed. The faint pulses in her feet could indicate a variety of things, one of which was that her body sensed it was in crisis and had begun to shut down blood vessels in the extremities, which aren't necessary to sustaining life. The body does this to ensure that the vital organs get what they need first.

Izmat seemed to have a fever, but there were no thermometers to be found. I gave five hundred milligrams of paracetomol, which is the European version of acetaminophen (Tylenol), and applied a wet towel with a couple of pieces of ice. The fever diminished over the shift.

I didn't know what her full diagnosis was, but one of the sisters told me that Izmat had a longstanding case of TB and liver disease (not further described). This could account for the blood she vomited. Paracetomol isn't great for the liver, but I was more afraid that she might spike a high fever, which could start the seizures again.

Later on I would find that one of the volunteers had fed the unconscious Izmat during the afternoon shift, which was another likely source of the fluid that filled her lung fields. At that point I didn't even have to use the stethoscope to know she had aspirated, which means fluid had run down her throat and into her lungs. I could feel the fluid bubbling in her chest when I laid my hand on it. So, once again I had to address the practice of force-feeding an unconscious patient. It's an age-old problem in hospice care because feeding a loved one is a primal instinct, but feeding an unconscious patient orally is dangerous. Food and drink tend to end up in the lungs when the patient is unable to purposefully swallow.

When air or food enter through the mouth, they travel through a passage called the laryngopharynx. At the end of the laryngopharynx is a little flap called the epiglottis. It closes when food is ingested, to route the food into the esophagus instead of the larynx, which is the passageway to the lungs. This all happens by reflex, and we don't even perceive it, but at the end of life the reflex may be vastly slowed or lost. When food and fluids go into the lungs, they cause all kinds of problems, such as pneumonia, not to mention that you can't breathe when the tissues are blocked by fluid. One day the doctor asked accusingly whether I would have them stop the force-feeding, and I said I would. I know he thought I was a murderer.

The other patient I feared might die that day was Mustafa, the man with varicella (chicken pox). Even without the thermometer, there was no question that his fever was high. He was panting and his eyes were fixed and staring half-open. It was a look I'd seen many times at hospice. All this told me he would die soon—maybe that night—and there was nothing I could do to stop it. Varicella is a virus, which does not respond to antibiotics, and we didn't have the antivirals, such as acyclovir, that fight the herpes strains. Though we had given him gentamycin, a strong antibiotic, to combat any secondary bacterial infection that might be attacking his body, it had made no difference.

Since varicella is highly contagious, I tried to find out which of the volunteers had had chicken pox. This did not turn out to be an easy task, due to language barriers, but I told them as best I could not to touch him unless they'd had the vaccine or disease.

Once again, I had to convince the volunteers in the men's ward to apply cool compresses rather than cover Mustafa in a wool blanket. When a patient has fever, piling on blankets actually increases body temperature—the reverse of what we want.

While I was there, the volunteers wanted me to insert IVs into two patients with wet, congested-sounding lungs. I refused, because I didn't want to add fluids to congested lungs. These volunteers were not health-care workers, and they seemed to think there was something magical about IV hydration. It was viewed as a final resort for patients at *Kalighat*, but intravenous fluids would do more harm than good to wet lungs, because their bodies were not efficiently ridding themselves of fluids, which was part of the reason their lungs got wet in the first place. Wet or swollen lung tissue does not allow oxygen to pass into the bloodstream efficiently, so you have to dry out the lungs, even at the risk of mild dehydration.

Everybody at *Kalighat* worked desperately to keep these people alive, which I applaud in concept. Unfortunately, we didn't always have the means to cure or to make the patients whom we couldn't cure as comfortable as I would have liked. The hospice nurse in me was conflicted about this, having seen that there are worse things on this earth than death.

Given the language barrier, I tried to explain my decision not to give IVs as best I could and get on to the other patients. Fortunately, I found a delightful young German man who helped me give the shots on the men's side. He was so kind to the patients and talked them through the shots, yet he also held the patients firmly in case anyone changed his mind. Some patients were combative, and I couldn't blame them. Not only were they ill, they had to drop their drawers so some strange Western woman could jab them in the rear with a needle. This really went against their cultural mores.

The issue of lack of pain control reared its ugly head again. On the way home, I heard that Kavita, Thomasina's burn patient, was being given an acetaminophen equivalent for what must have been agony. Considering that everyone seemed to fear addicting the patients here, and also considering how common this same attitude is among doctors and nurses in the States, I shouldn't have been shocked, but I was. I have strong feelings about providing relief from pain, and abundant research shows that patients who are properly treated for pain rarely become addicted. In fact, for decades studies have consistently shown that less than a fraction of one percent of such patients become addicted.

While tolerance to opioids does build over time, once the pain is under control, the doses can be reduced in increments to prevent symptoms of withdrawal and there will be no addiction. When pain is properly controlled, the patient is also less likely to overmedicate himself, as happens in poorly controlled pain. Doctors now recognize a syndrome called pseudoaddiction, which is drug-seeking behavior caused by inadequate pain control.[22] These patients are the proverbial "clock-watchers," who ring the nurse call bell the moment it's time for their medications. They will hoard medications for times when their pain is too much, which is one of the ways they end up overmedicated. They also shop around at different doctors' offices and obtain multiple prescriptions, because what they're taking doesn't stop their pain. The difference between this behavior and true addiction is that when pain is adequately controlled, the pseudoaddict's drug-seeking behavior goes away.

Again, I can only guess that having narcotics on hand might make all Missionaries of Charity facilities targets for theft and put everyone in danger. In February of 2004, Mother Teresa's successor, Sister Nirmala, was robbed in the Indian countryside, and she had nothing as tempting as drugs to give the robbers.

Of course, drug availability was not a problem for all patients, quite the contrary in fact. Anjali, the girl who had been beaten and raped, was offered the medications she needed but continued to spit them out. I didn't even know whether she had been eating, since there was no patient chart or shift report. Plus, we scurried about so much in nursing that sometimes we didn't even get to talk to each other during a shift.

Anjali could also be quite wild and hit people who came near her. I ended up giving her an injection of the light tranquilizer diazepam to calm her. At least it helped her sleep.

The Indian employees yelled at her for not taking her medicine. I guess it was cultural for them to yell. I'd seen people interact that way on the street, but that didn't mean I understood it. On the other hand, I didn't think there was anyone unkind working at Mother Teresa's, and from what I could tell, the patients did not take it the same way we would in America.

Meanwhile, I was having more problems with people believing I was a doctor. Anuradha, the paralyzed woman I catheterized, told me through an interpreter that she would see no one else but me for medical treatment in the future, because I was the only one who healed her pain. She had a four-year-old son and said she'd bring him to me for medical care as well. She was little more than a child herself, and she stared at me with hope in her eyes as I went about my business in the ward. I was unnerved by her faith and at a loss as to what to do about it. That morning she'd asked me to look at her spinal X-ray. Fortunately, a report accompanied it and there was nothing in the image to make me disagree with the report. I'm no expert. I simply could not convince her of that.

Deepika, the dwarf, whose infected finger I lanced, now showed me the finger several times a day. It had healed. She had been so angry with me when I lanced it that I thought she would never speak to me again.

I wished I were worthy of such trust, but reality won out a few days later when Izmat died. She slipped into a coma after a night of seizures and vomiting blood, but roused for a day and spent the afternoon with her family gathered around her. Her sister, mother, and a young male child sat around her wearing brightly colored clothing. They brought in food and fed Izmat. They all laughed, and Izmat enjoyed the child's antics.

The next evening she slipped into a coma and died. I went against my own common sense when I suggested an IV after she lapsed back into coma, but I thought she had a chance of survival and hoped the extra fluids would revive her enough to sit up and eat again. Not knowing the diagnosis certainly made such decisions harder. Still, all you really have in medicine are educated guesses, gut feelings, and playing the odds. I knew it was not impossible for her to improve, but both my gut and the odds were against it. Truth be told, I really wanted to be wrong.

It is rare, but I'd seen other dying patients wake up for a short period of time to say goodbye to loved ones. It is also common for dying patients who are not in a coma to experience a last surge of energy.

A woman I took care of in a hospice years ago, a cancer patient in her seventies, had been unconscious in another hospital. Once it was determined that she would probably not regain consciousness, she was admitted to our hospice for terminal care. She had requested that her life not be extended by artificial means, so the hospital had not given IV nutrition for a week, and she was not expected to last much longer.

One morning I came in and began to clean her mouth, a comfort measure that can be carried out whether the patient is conscious or not. As I swabbed out the dried tissue, I spoke to her, explaining everything I was doing. It is well known that comatose patients hear and feel, so hospice nurses talk to their patients, even as they wash the body in preparation for transport to the mortuary. Anyway, I had just finished applying a lubricant to her lips when she opened her eyes and asked, "Have you got any strawberry ice cream?"

I ran to the phone and told her family to come quickly. Soon, family and friends began to pour in. They brought her favorite music and foods, and one heck of a party ensued. At one point, when everyone was crowded around the stack of CDs they'd brought, trying to figure out what to play next, I happened to look over at the patient. She was lying in bed with her arms stretched to heaven. There was a smile on her face and her lips were moving. After the party, she said goodbye to everyone, slipped into another coma, and did not regain consciousness. She died two days later.

BENGALI NEW YEAR AND CHRISTIAN HOPE

We celebrated Easter mass at *Kalighat* today. In his sermon, the priest reminded us of Corrie ten Boom, a Dutch Christian woman whose family helped hide Jewish families during the Nazi occupation of the Netherlands. When the Nazis came to their door, her father, who did not believe in telling lies, revealed their secret. She and her entire family were arrested and interned in concentration camps. Most of her relatives died. She survived to write and lecture extensively on forgiveness. It occurred to me that people who could offer that level of forgiveness were all around me at *Kalighat*, but I'm not sure I'm one of them.

Easter coincided with the festivities for the Bengali New Year, and all kinds of music—cymbals and drums mostly—blasted in from the street as a backdrop for mass. It is the Indian tradition to give alms and to wear new clothes to start the year. In honor of this, one Bengali family brought in dinner and another brought lunch, and all the patients got new outfits.

A point of interest to me was that the Bengalis use a different calendar to track the years. The year 2004 was 1411 on the Bengali calendar. The New Year is called *Poila Boisakh—poila* meaning "first" and *Boisakh*, the first month.

During the Bengali New Year celebration, people create beautiful designs on their floors with colored rice powder. The centerpiece of the design is an earthenware pot filled with water and a stem of mango leaves. The outside of the pot is decorated with a red and white swastika to symbolize good fortune for the family in the coming year. The swastika is sometimes shown in the palm of the chubby elephant god Ganesha's right hand to symbolize luck. While it is shocking for a Westerner to see, the swastika appears in ancient Indian architecture, long predating the Nazis' use of its reversed image.

The Bengali New Year was quite an experience at *Kalighat*, since it was located adjacent to the Kali Temple, a central focus of the New Year celebration. Representations of Kali were sold everywhere on the street. She is the frightening-looking goddess with an extra eye in the middle of her forehead and a long crimson tongue that extends from her mouth like a snake. She has four arms: one with a sword; one with a severed head; and two raised in praise. She is usually depicted wearing a necklace of skulls and a belt of severed arms. One disturbing thing for me to learn was that they sacrifice goats to her at the Kali Temple daily.

Phillis said that monks and opportunists masquerading as monks (it's hard for foreigners to tell which is which) give fascinating tours of the Kali Temple. When you leave, though, the charlatans ask you to donate one thousand five hundred rupees, a huge amount by local standards. Fifty rupees is a fine donation, and you should pay no more than that. Phillis had a guidebook that had warned of this ploy.

I preferred the more peaceful image that I encountered at Mother Teresa's house. During the break between the morning and afternoon shifts, I sat out on the balcony of *Kalighat* with the sisters praying in a room to my right and the sounds of the street bazaar on my left. I took off my shoes to dry my socks, and put my feet up to relax.

My favorite black birds watched from surrounding buildings. They blended with the sooty look of the stuccoed facades. I'd been told they were of the crow family, and their cawing certainly supported that. Their coloring, however, was quite distinctive. They had gray heads, save the foreheads, mouths and the ring around their necks; the rest was a sooty black.

On the exterior wall that overlooked the balcony was a large crucifix with the words "I thirst" written on a plaque at Christ's feet. This statement is the traditional accompaniment to the crucifixes in all the Missionaries of Charity houses. During a speech she gave at the National Prayer Breakfast in Washington, D.C., Mother Teresa said,

When He was dying on the cross, Jesus said, "I thirst." Jesus is thirsting for our love, and this is the thirst of everyone, poor and rich alike. We all thirst for the love of others, that they go out of their way to avoid harming us and to do good to us. This is the meaning of true love, to give until it hurts.[23]

Behind the crucifix were giant cupolas with four smaller cupolas around each. I wondered whether this architecture originated in India and was transported to the Slavic countries, where the onion dome graces so many buildings. If so, how? I'm sure war had something to do with it.

A huge black butterfly with white spots flitted by the painful image of Christ on the cross, and I was reminded of what I learned years ago at hospice—even in death, even when disease has distorted the face and body, there is beauty. You just have to look for it. It could be the eyes or hair or hands, but there is always something that death and disease cannot take.

From my seat on the balcony, I could see formerly grand houses on three sides and the ornate Kali Temple at the back. The Kali Temple had a silver roof and a tall steeple with layers of various colors adorning the base. The art inside the temple was supposed to be of brilliant color as well. It was a thought-provoking contrast to the simplicity of the sisters and the facilities on our side of the wall.

I enjoyed sitting in the sun and thinking quiet thoughts, but I was feeling faint and regretted not bringing extra water. I hadn't brought anything with me because I had not planned to stay the afternoon. Even so, I found it hard to turn the sisters down if they needed anything, and no other nurses were scheduled to come in, so there I sat. For the past few days I'd been eating as many bananas as possible because I thought I was getting dehydrated and needed the potassium. Nevertheless, I had been getting dizzy earlier in the day when I crouched down, which was my normal work stance next to the cots.

One of the sisters taught me a trick for detecting dehydration: examine the tongue. Fissures indicate dehydration. I thought to myself that I'd have to look at mine the next time I was around a mirror and sufficient light, because some of the signs I had been taught to rely upon in the United States didn't necessarily work in Kolkata's constant heat. Urinary output, for example, was characteristically low for active people in Kolkata—even after drinking several liters of water in a day. I guessed this was the body's way of compensating for fluids lost through perspiration. Nonetheless, I pledged to drink more fluids and pay more attention to what my body needed so I could keep working.

I didn't want to be unreliable for the sisters. Their work was difficult, although Sister Georgina, who was in charge of the *Kalighat* facility, displayed a wonderful attitude that would lead one to think she never minded the work. She was tall and caramel-colored, and her voice was soft. No matter what, she looked calm in the worst of storms. She said there was no use getting upset about things, because we could put our trust in God to provide. The evidence was in her favor according to what I saw at *Kalighat*.

Her words were simple and true. Why could I not follow them? All I could wonder was, were these sisters really so confident that God would provide? And why did I feel that it was my responsibility to heal when it was really God calling the shots? I was just a nurse who was trying to do the right thing. I was no match for the faith the sisters held.

Having never been around nuns, I hadn't known what to expect, but I'd been pleasantly surprised and looked forward to seeing them every day. A nun who really touched me was Sister Lumen. A nurse from America, her accent hinted at Irish influence. On the mornings when we rode out into the countryside to set up one-day dispensaries for those who couldn't get to Kolkata for medical care, Sister Lumen led prayer and songs throughout the trip. I noted how much she enjoyed singing rounds and harmonies, which often sent her into peals of laughter. A diminutive woman, she had a warm smile and a presence that commanded respect without asking.

Sister Georgina and *Kalighat's* sole fulltime professional nurse, Sister Pei Ling, reminded me of the Rudyard Kipling poem "If": "If you can keep your head when all about you are losing theirs..."

It is not fair to say I had a favorite, because they were all so nice, despite the frantic pace they keep, but I still think of Sister Lumen as my friend. She said she'd give me the names of some sisters in Baltimore so that I could volunteer as a nurse at Gift of Hope, the Missionaries of Charity AIDS home near the Johns Hopkins Hospital. That would serve the purpose of being a volunteer and coincidentally solve my problem of having to nurse a certain number of hours to keep my license. What struck me most about this sister was that her joy glowed. I would call her smile luminous.

Sister Michael, a doctor who attended mostly to the health of the other sisters and led the dispensaries in the countryside, was tall and fair with a warm, easy smile. She was gentle and meek but knew her stuff.

I'd seen how she took time with the patients and listened, even as people crowded around her and pulled at her to gain her attention.

Though all the novices received a certain amount of medical training, Sister Pei Ling was the only formally educated nurse permanently assigned to *Kalighat*. She was at the center of all activity. If I had her job, I'd be screaming at the end of the day because little took place in the house that didn't end up involving her. She was the only one who knew how to decipher the babble of pharmaceuticals that had been donated by various countries, and she alone knew the hiding place of certain valuable medical supplies that had been targeted for theft in the past.

The novices hailed mainly from Africa and India, with a few from the West, but their accents were amazingly consistent when they prayed and sang. Their songs evoked innocence and joy, and they were always eager to learn nursing skills. The novices were like little angels in their plain white sari robes, but one tall sister particularly amused me. Of sturdy stock, she could put on a stern look, so she ended up being the gate guard and crowd controller. The other sisters loved her, and I watched them play a joke on her when she fell asleep during devotions on the truck. One by one, the novices noticed she was asleep. A contagion of rib poking and pointing rippled through the group. With a few giggles, one of the sisters started a lively, hand-clapping hymn, and they sang and clapped much louder than usual, all eyes riveted to the sleeping sister. When at last she awoke, it was not with a start. Her lips pursed before her eyes slowly opened, and everyone dissolved into laughter. It had been a long time since I'd experienced such tender merriment.

One image I'll carry of the Missionaries of Charity is of bare feet, feet that are kept as clean as possible but show signs of physical work. Most of the missionaries are tiny women with little feet. When the sisters kneeled, their toes peeked out from beneath the saris. When they walked, they moved in silence. Mother's feet were gnarled with age, the toes twisted from bunions and wrinkled with time.

I've been pondering the phenomenon that married men live significantly longer than single men, but a woman's life expectancy is more tied to the presence of strong bonds with other females. I think these sisters will have long lives indeed.

DOCTORS IN THE HOUSE

People were packed into every corner of the bus, and the hot season was in full swing. They clung to any available support, but there were ladies' seats that weren't taken, so I was able to sit.

The air on the buses was stifling, even though the windows had no glass and were open, except for a couple of wooden slats nailed horizontally across them. As the buses approached the stops, the ticket sellers hung out the door and rattled off every stop like auctioneers. Many of them recognized those of us who were on our way to *Kalighat*. When they spotted us they shouted, "*Kalighat, Kalighat, Kalighat,*" in rapid-fire succession. It became a joke among volunteers to greet each other by spouting "*Kalighat, Kalighat, Kalighat,*" as fast as we could.

Because of the New Year season, the *Kalighat* Market was more of a gauntlet than usual. There were gates channeling hundreds into the Kali Temple and beggars lined every step of the route. As we approached the temple area, the beggars became more aggressive. It was obvious that they expected us all to donate during the New Year holiday.

The sun bored through gelatinous humidity as Carolyn and I went off through the market to buy cups for the patients at *Kalighat*. We were running low on the wards. The vendors wanted ten times what they were worth, so we walked away. Too bad for the vendors—I would have bought twenty, but they were so greedy that they ended up with nothing. I'm sure they thought they would sell a lot of cups that day, because the weather was hot and the market was crowded with people waiting to get into the temple, but I was also sure they wouldn't have asked Indians to pay what they asked of us. After hitting a few stalls and getting the same runaround, I decided to give my money to one of the Indian women in *Kalighat*'s kitchen and ask her to negotiate the price.

Slightly dejected, we entered *Kalighat* without our gifts, but what waited for us was a wonderful surprise. Three American doctors from Oregon had come to volunteer for the day—I'll call them Liz, Mark, and David. Apparently they spent their spare time working with doctors in Third World countries. They had also visited a medical school in Kenya and said that the Kenyan medical school hospital was on a par with what they saw at *Kalighat*.

Liz sharps-debrided Kshama, a rather wild woman who I thought had a staph infection. Liz said it was hard to determine what caused the infection in the absence of lab reports. She said it had the look of a mycobacterium, which includes tuberculosis, but there could have been any of a number of causes. Later in the shift, Liz found Kshama trying to climb out a window and suggested a trial of the antipsychotic haloperidol, which worked wonders.

Liz also examined Anuradha, the woman who could not move her legs. The neurological exam was a process of elimination, testing how much the patient was able to feel and where. She used her hands to feel for structural damage and areas of tenderness. The spinal exam didn't show any remarkable damage, such as broken bones or slipped disks, and the patient did not express discomfort as Liz probed her back and legs.

Through an interpreter, Liz focused on which direction the loss of sensation had moved (top to bottom or bottom to top), and whether it had been progressive or sudden. Spinal lesions often cause a rapid loss of sensation that is top to bottom. The other disease Liz initially suspected was Guillain-Barré syndrome, an inflammatory polyneuropathy (meaning inflammation of many nerves) that causes a paralysis that is sometimes temporary. The most common form of Guillain-Barré is known as "ascending," because the weakness and numbness begin in the legs and ascend. We are not certain what causes Guillain-Barré, but it is thought to be an autoimmune response to a viral infection. Guillain-Barré became notorious in the 1970s, because an outbreak of the disease followed swine flu vaccinations. Urinary retention is common in Guillain-Barré, which was consistent with Anuradha's need for a catheter.

After conducting the best neurological exam and interview she could through the non-medically trained interpreter, Liz thought it was most likely Guillain-Barré syndrome. I prayed she was right because—though it can mean permanent paralysis or even death from respiratory failure—the effects of Guillain-Barré can reverse after a period of time, usually six months to a year. Still, we couldn't confirm this without laboratory tests, and the Indian doctor decided on a trial of steroids instead of sending her out for such tests.

I was to learn later, steroids may sometimes reduce inflammation in Guillain-Barré, but their curative effect is questionable. More effective is plasmapheresis, a high-tech process wherein blood is removed, filtered of certain proteins, then mixed with fresh frozen plasma or a solution with a chemical balance that is similar to the blood's, and transfused back to the patient. This only works within the first couple of weeks after the onset of Guillain-Barré—otherwise, there is nothing to do but treat what symptoms you can and hope it reverses.

After examining the rape victim Anjali, Liz's main concern was the potential for sexually transmitted disease. We went to the medicine cabinet together and found Rocefin, an antibiotic that would combat sexually transmitted disease with only one injection. Thank God, because we only had three doses in the house. As an added benefit, the serum came in a powder form that was to be reconstituted with the local anesthetic lidocaine, so after the initial jab, Anjali would feel nothing.

Liz held the girl while I gave the shot. Anjali didn't like being restrained, and I felt terrible hurting this child, even though it was in her best interest, but this is why I don't work in pediatrics. In the end, I knew it was the most prudent thing we could do, because Anjali was still refusing oral antibiotics when she felt like it. The clothes I'd worn the day before had gone to the laundry spattered with the gummy capsules she'd spit on me.

Mark and David were also wonderful to work with. They found a case of cutaneous leishmaniasis in the men's ward. Spread by the bite of the sand fly, leishmaniasis can be cutaneous, which means sores appear on the skin, or visceral, which means it affects organs, such as the spleen. Cutaneous leishmaniasis can be chronic, but visceral leishmaniasis is often fatal. One characteristic of the wounds on the skin is that they tend to look like volcanoes with their cratered centers.

Next, we had some adventures looking through the medicine cabinet to find an injectable antibiotic that was appropriate for a man who had just been brought in with a case of what David and Mark suspected was pneumonia. The man was in his early twenties and was vocalizing with each pant in sort of a soft scream. His eyes darted back and forth, and he was obviously panicked. On top of that, he was panting his way into respiratory alkalosis, which might be fatal if we couldn't get him calmed down. His feet were cool and seemed to be mottled, a sign of oxygen deprivation and often a harbinger of death. Mottling is a change in skin tone that appears as spots of blue to purple on pale skin and darker tones on dark skin. It often begins on the soles of the feet, but it is difficult to distinguish hues on the sole of a foot that hasn't worn shoes in a while. The calluses obscure the color changes, which are harder to discern on darker pigmentation anyway.

Attending to the panting was the first order of business. Respiratory alkalosis is a condition caused by chemical imbalance, in which the body essentially loses the urge to take in oxygen. In the advanced stage, it slows breathing to a full stop. When a person breathes at a rapid and shallow rate—panting—he blows off all the carbon dioxide. Breathing is triggered when carbon dioxide builds up in the lungs and the lungs work to exchange it for oxygen. Panting gets rid of the carbon dioxide and the lungs think they don't need to take a breath. This is why we had to take care of the panting first.

We decided on IV diazepam to soothe him and hopefully get the breathing under control. I pushed it slowly into his IV and, yes, his breathing calmed immediately, so much so that I sat by the bed for a while to make sure it wasn't going to stop altogether. It happened so suddenly that I contemplated the ethics of performing CPR on a desperately ill person who was not likely to recover. I'd also be putting myself in jeopardy of catching whatever disease he had, because there was no other means available to restart the breathing except unprotected mouth-to-mouth.

As I wrestled with my conscience, his breathing bottomed out and began to come up again. I watched him breathe until I was satisfied that he was stable enough to leave him, then wiped my sweating brow—this time from anxiety—and went back to the women's side.

As I rounded the corner of the women's ward, I heard Liz telling the European nurse Thomasina to discontinue poor burned Kavita's diuretic, because Kavita's legs were swelling from loss of albumin caused by the burns, and the lasix would just get rid of more electrolytes and throw her heart into crisis. Since Liz was a doctor, Thomasina obeyed. Thank God for Liz.

When I returned in the afternoon, I let the other nurses care for the patients while I sorted newly donated medicines. The drugs were stored in wooden boxes that were marked with some general categories of usage such as "stomach upset." My task was to sort drugs into these categories. Perhaps it was a sign of the patient population's lack of access to medical diagnostics, but there were no boxes for heart and blood pressure medications. As I dropped the heart and blood pressure medications into the "Odds" box, I contemplated why. In the United States, a huge sector of the population takes cardiovascular drugs, and I would have thought that people of a similar age in India would be taking them too. After considering this, I realized that the people of the streets couldn't get annual checkups or have their blood pressure monitored on a regular basis. It's just another thing I had taken for granted when I viewed the situation through American eyes.

Generally, pharmaceutical products were dirt cheap in India, but that's not as good as it sounds. I was speaking with an Argentine nurse named Julio about a patient who was not responding to a particular antibiotic therapy. Julio asked me where the antibiotic had been manufactured, then told me you can't be sure what you are buying in some countries, and India is one of them. I later found a World Health Organization study on the Internet that said, "Up to 25% of the medicines consumed in poor countries are counterfeit or substandard...figures place the annual earnings from the sales of counterfeit and substandard medicines at over US$32 billion globally."[24]

My friend Phillis, an engineer in one of the world's largest pharmaceutical companies, explained why medications cost so much in the United States. The Federal Drug Administration process is quite lengthy, and the drug must not only pass multi-phased trials, the production engineering process itself must be tested and approved to assure equal distribution of drug throughout a product, as well as consistency in quality during production. The layout of the production plant is part of the approval process. Once approved, the plant's process cannot be changed for the life of the product without going through another round of approvals. Meanwhile, precious years tick away on the patent clock.

Drug companies survive by discovery and must always have newly developed drugs in the pipeline. Once the patent runs out and a product becomes generic, those who have not borne the cost of the research can get the chemical formulation and sell it. Other countries do not require these strict controls, so the drugs can be sold more cheaply. Phillis said that, while drugs sold in other countries may be quality drugs, you could count on consistency and quality in the drugs manufactured for the United States.

Sometimes the curative agents are not pharmaceutical at all. A man came in with deep wounds in his calf. Maggots had eaten away half the gastrosnemus muscle, and when Thomasina poured an iodine and saline solution into it, hundreds of maggots—and I'm not exaggerating—came running out. I must say, once they'd been cleared out, I could see that the maggots had left a nice, clean wound. It's possible that they saved him from a below-the-knee amputation. Nonetheless, I've heard that the nerve pain they create is horrible, and I'm sure that the feeling of having them move in your body is maddening.

A French nurse told me that they use maggots and leeches in their medical practice, but that you have to watch the beasts carefully. While their initial action is beneficial in that they eat necrotic tissue, left to their own devices, they will continue to feed on the good tissue as well. This man's wounds would have to be cleaned again and again as the days wore on, because it was likely that more maggots would hatch.

The American doctors who had volunteered in the morning commented that they were viewed in the hospital where they were on sabbatical as having "new ideas" and "new methods." This was not meant as a compliment. They noted that the academic learning among the Indian doctors in Kolkata is profound, but bridging the gap from excellent academic performance to practice on humans was not accomplished as well as would have been expected based upon the academics. Also, the facilities were terrible. It was not unusual, for instance, to see an animal walking through a ward.

Regulation of doctors in this overpopulated country was slipshod. The Hindustan Times ran an article one day entitled, "Fake doctor arrested after child's death."[25] Apparently, a man was masquerading as a cardiologist but had only a tenth-grade education. This charlatan was so successful that he had offices in ten locations and influential friends in various medical colleges. When a child under his care became jaundiced and died from liver disease, the child's father took his records to another physician, who suspected fraud when he saw what medications the quack had prescribed.

Another headline read: "RS 25 Lakhs [25,000,000 rupees] to be a Doc! Pay a premium to get into a medical college through a donor seat."[26] The article exposed several Indian medical schools that sell admission to donors.

While he could be quite charming, *Kalighat's* volunteer Indian doctor's view of Western healthcare providers was not what I would have expected. He told me the real purpose of *Kalighat* was to teach the volunteers humility, an interesting perspective from a person who had shown none. I knew that Mother Teresa wanted us to learn what it is like to be Indian and to live as the poor. Nonetheless, I don't think Mother saw teaching Westerners humility as the main reason for establishing the homes. I do think the doctor's anger about Western medical volunteers and their "new ideas" was showing through. He seemed especially disdainful in his judgment that we Westerners could not change anything. I guessed that was why he preferred to criticize the Western nurses than to consider that there might be merit in what we had to say. Perhaps he believed in predetermined life. I saw a lot of the attitude that man can do nothing to change his lot in life because whatever happens is meant to be. It took me back to my Presbyterian childhood roots and to ideas I heard long before I joined Martin Luther's church.

It was John Calvin who developed the philosophy of predestination, and my understanding of it is, essentially, that some people are predestined or chosen by God and others are not. Part of his point was that we cannot earn what is freely given, but the concept is so tinged with the implication that God intentionally excludes people from salvation that many Presbyterians, including me, can't embrace it. Similarly, I am not able to understand the Buddhist influence in Indian culture that advises man to accept suffering and attain detachment from desire to achieve contentment. I guess I'm too much of an activist for that.

In Kolkata, where the Communist Party was strong, there is an obstinate distrust of the West. This lesson was learned during colonial days and perpetuated through the old Soviet "Active Measures" propaganda program. The Indian doctor told me that the anti-U.S. propaganda had been so effective in Soviet days that some of the people in India actually believed the United States could control the weather and thus blamed us for droughts, floods, and famine. Instead of looking at food distribution problems in their own country, they were convinced that Americans took an unfair amount of the world's food and thereby created starvation in poorer nations. While this attitude does not persist in the majority of Indians, those who have little contact with the outside world still feel suspicious. That could account for some of my mistreatment at the hands of cab drivers.

Yet my concerns focused on the here and now: could the doctor at *Kalighat* relieve these patients' suffering, and would his care be tainted with prejudice against accepting the advice of Western nurses? I'd seen him take Carolyn to task when he insisted she had said something she had not. He had simply misunderstood her, and he not only launched into a temper tantrum and wouldn't allow her to explain, he refused to even look at her patient after that.

I was also angry that he did not actually examine the patients. He stood off several feet from the beds and asked questions of those patients who'd been pointed out to him as having special problems. He did not touch them or show an interest in those about whom the nuns and nurses had said nothing. On top of that, he was hypersensitive if you questioned anything he said, and I've found in the medical field that if a doctor or nurse becomes angry when you ask questions, it's probably because they don't know the answer and are embarrassed to admit it.

I had even wondered whether he was a medical doctor or a doctor of one of the traditional medical arts, because I sure didn't understand how he came to some of his conclusions. Lavanya, the physical therapist with the shin ulcers so deep they revealed muscle, complained of vaginal itching. The Indian doctor conducted a gynecological "exam" while he stood at least four feet away and asked her to hold herself open. Of course this was without any modesty draping and in the middle of the open ward. Considering the dress requirements for women in India, what must she have felt like? Anyway, after peering at her genitals from afar he told me to put an antibiotic on her labia (lips of the vagina). Knowing that she might itch even though her exterior tissues looked normal, I reminded him that we had vaginal creams. In an irritated tone, he insisted that I use an antibiotic. Lavanya had been on antibiotics, and a female patient on antibiotics who had develops vaginal itching is a classic picture of a patient with *candidiasis*, also known as a yeast infection. This is basic knowledge for any woman, much less a doctor. The treatment is an antifungal, not more antibiotic, which kills bacteria indiscriminately and likely caused the problem in the first place. Also, Lavanya was a diabetic, and diabetics are plagued with vaginal yeast infections due to their disease process. *Candidiasis* should have been his first suspicion. I waited until he left and applied the vaginal cream, then went out and bought her a dose of oral flucanazole.

I tried hard to remember that different does not equate to wrong, but in the weeks that followed, I fumed over this doctor's decisions. For example, he wanted to start a patient on an inhaler for a respiratory condition. The patient did not want to take the medicine, so the doctor told me to force him, explaining that the man had no frame of reference for the inhaler and could not understand that it wouldn't hurt him. I tried again to persuade the man, but he still refused.

The doctor grumbled that the inhaler was as foreign to this man as a space ship and that the man was too simple to understand. He then had a couple of volunteers hold the patient while he forced a couple of puffs into the man's mouth. Aside from the obvious harshness of method, an inhaler must be *inhaled* into the lungs, not just sprayed into the mouth. It actually takes training and a bit of coordination to use an inhaler because you have to keep your tongue down, breathe in as you spray, and hold your breath for a couple of seconds. All that the doctor accomplished by forcing the patient was to scare him. But the doctor had the power to ban me from the House, so I often avoided confrontation and said, "Yes sir, yes sir, three bags full," then went about my business for the couple of hours a week he was there.

A SICK DAY

It was time to wash the day's accumulation of grime off my face and body. Most nights when I returned to my hotel, the dirt was visible, often tangible, as when particles fell into my mouth during yawns and were crushed between my teeth before I realized they were there. If I sat on my bed before showering and changing clothes, I left charcoal-gray marks on the sheets. My toenails, which are normally pedicured, looked like I'd been walking through a barbecue pit. My fingernails were only slightly better, despite my medical handwashing routine. There were many things I'd grown accustomed to on this trip. The sight of dirt embedded in my hands when I touched a patient was not one of them.

The good news was that the shoes I bought on the shopping trip with Phillis and Margaret had turned out to be a total godsend. They had gel-like soles with a little bounce. What a relief! I'd been concerned that the macerated tissues of my feet harbored something untoward that I wouldn't recognize until my skin started falling off, but my feet felt entirely renewed after they dried out a bit.

The bad news was that I had become ill during the afternoon shift and had had to leave *Kalighat* early. About mid-morning I noticed a slight soreness that felt kind of like a dry throat. By afternoon it was terrible. I felt faint, and I also felt like my throat was swelling shut, plus, I had pain in the right side of my chest up around the bronchial passages.

I had drunk two liters of water before this all happened, but the temperature was thirty-seven degrees Celsius, which is ninety-eight-point six degrees Fahrenheit, and there were only a few ceiling fans to keep us cool as we worked on the patients. I supposed that the faintness could have come from dehydration, but I feared it was related to the sore throat, so I decided to go to bed early to relax, read the newspapers, and record thoughts in my journal.

I found the local papers quite entertaining to read. The Indians enjoy the turn of the phrase in their headlines. They tend to be playful in their phraseology, using titles like you see in American high school sports pages: "Cong bays for Modi's blood," meaning that congress wanted a chief minister to resign. It was a fun game to attempt to guess what such titles meant before reading the article.

The election news was also fascinating. That evening, there was a quote from a parliamentary aspirant, who had recently been revealed as being Pakistani. He had sworn in his application to run for office that he was Indian, but after a tip from a neighbor, his papers were reexamined and found to be false. He vowed to protest the finding and said in his own defense: "I have never visited Pakistan. I hate Pakistan. I love India and Indian democracy."

Other stories reinforced the differences between life in the U.S. and India. Almost as if it were an expected occurrence, a blurb stated simply: "A honey collector and a schoolgirl were mauled to death by tigers in the 24 Parganas while a leopard was killed by villagers in Bankura."

The banner headline in the world section of the day's *Hindustan Times* read: "Tom and Nicole rematch is fans' desire." What a strange topic for world news, especially considering the wars that were raging in the Middle East and closer to India, in Kashmir. In general, I was surprised to find that entertainment and leisure topics took such substantial space in the national newspapers. In fact, the papers were always full of pictures and tidbits about American film stars. The women were scantily clad—again a stark contrast to the culture in Kolkata, where even prostitutes did not wear such revealing clothing in public. The photographs made American women look immoral compared to Indian women, and this had to encourage men to assume we are.

I fell asleep in my clothes around seven in the evening and got the bed all dirty. So, when I awoke around one o'clock, I got up and took a shower. I also started azithromycin tablets for my sore throat. Getting sick in the tropics was a little scary because there were many diseases I hadn't encountered in the United States, as had been made painfully clear by the recent SARS epidemics, and I had no idea what I might have breathed into my lungs. I was certain I'd been exposed to strep recently, and heaven knows what strain the pneumonia patient carried—the one who had almost stopped breathing when I gave diazepam. Also, the fact that I had pain in my chest left me with a nagging fear of tuberculosis. Compounding the problem was that, without my pharmacy reference book, I was not particularly knowledgeable about when to use which antibiotic, because they are developed to combat specific types of organisms. However, I remembered that azithromycin attacks Gram-positive organisms, such as staph and strep, as well as a wide range of things that attack the ear, nose, throat, and respiratory system. It is also useful against other diseases, so it was worth a try.

Unable to sleep after my shower, I turned on the television. From the screen a sitar blared, but soon came the announcement that Stephen King's *Carrie* was coming on next. This was a typical daily contrast between where I was and where I was born.

Carrie is a story of shocking inhumanity, but it is an inhumanity borne of having little of substance to worry about, a wealth that obliterates the struggle to survive and propels some people to focus on harming others for the fun of it. It is an extreme form of waste. Poverty in the United States does not explain our sub-culture of violence, which we glorify in our movies and games. In India, some of the cruelty stems from culture, such as the practice of burning a wife to death so that the husband can remarry and get another dowry from a new wife's family. And there are also remnants of the Hindu caste system, which deems *Dalits*, members of the lowest caste, also known as the untouchables, as subhuman.

While the caste system was banned in 1950 with the signing of the Indian Constitution, human rights abuses against the *Dalits* abound in contemporary times. *Dalits* make up almost ninety percent of the destitute in India and they are frequent targets of crime that may be condoned or even perpetrated by law enforcement. This continues despite the 1989 act called *The Scheduled Castes and the Scheduled Tribes (Prevention of Atrocities) Act*, which criminalizes parading people naked through the streets, forcing them to eat inedible substances (feces being a common one), unjustly confiscating their land, fouling their water, burning their houses, raping women, and in the case of the police, failing to investigate victims' claims, among other things.[27] The act was largely to protect *Dalits*, who were commonly victimized by these crimes. In reality, physical and sexual assaults on *Dalit* women, sometimes by gangs of men, are still rarely investigated. Later, I was even to read that higher castes forced *Dalits* out of refugee camps for victims of the tsunami that hit in December 2004.

Another factor that proffered violence in Kolkata was desperation and impoverished living conditions—thirteen million people crowded into a space that cannot possibly provide resources for them to live in comfort. This sort of thing spurs cruelty of monumental proportions. In April, two boys entered a building and allegedly tried to steal a water pump. Neighbors heard screams at about four in the morning and ran out to find the owner of the pump and others beating the boys with iron rods. One of the boys passed out, so the crowd revived him with water and started in again. One boy was saved by his father, but the other died in the middle of the road after an hour of torture.

After watching *Carrie*, I drifted off to sleep, only to be awakened by a bug crawling on my neck. When it happened the first time, I flailed my arms to get rid of the beast and reach the light switch. In the process, I hit the call button on the bedside stand. The button was designed to chime a rendition of *Für Elise*, but over the period of time that I'd been at the hotel, something had gone wrong with the bell system, leaving it out of tune and rather manic. It seemed to not just to be off-key but schizophrenic, with one bell communicating a fainter chord that didn't belong. It was as if one bell followed each note a fraction of a second off, like a discordant grace note.

The waiter came to the room, and without opening the door I convinced him to go, but I couldn't go back to sleep. Every time the fan blew my hair, I feared it was another insect. My mind was playing tricks on me. The first couple of nights, I'd experienced itching every time I went to bed. When I put a plastic cover on the mattress, the itching stopped. Thanks to advice I'd found on the Internet at an Irish volunteer site, I'd brought the cover with me but had thought it would not be necessary in such a nice hotel. I still don't know whether the itch was from an allergy to something in the materials or from bedbugs.

Later that night, I found another creepy crawler. To my relief, it was just a roach. Whoever thought that would be a comfort? *Just* a roach. I wished there were some way to hang the mosquito netting I'd brought, but there wasn't.

Though the room wasn't large enough to spread the furniture out, I moved the bed away from the wall and other furniture as much as possible. I'd been told that the extra space would make it a little harder for bugs to jump from the wall or other furniture onto the bed. I also ensured that the bedclothes were tucked in, so crawling insects couldn't climb up the sheets from the floor. I even shook my shoes before I put them on in the mornings, as I had at summer camp in Texas, where scorpions were known to secret themselves in the dark recesses of shoes at night.

Don't get me wrong—the hotel room was nice, but some things about it were mystifying. It shook at intervals, like bridges do when they bear heavy traffic. Also, there were approximately twelve electrical switches in the room and three others in the hall that controlled the room. Of the switches inside the room, four said "lamp," and I'd been told that the largest lever was the power to the hot water heater. One plate said "tube," which I assumed meant the television, and another said "fan," yet it did not control the fan. I had no idea what the rest were for.

There was a radio that didn't work but was a fine telephone stand. The lights were those coiled long-life bulbs, and they had no shades. "Off" was up on light switches, and faucets turned in the opposite direction from those in the United States.

The view from my windows was nothing to write home about. Aside from the backs of buildings, I could see corrugated roofs—gray-black of course—scattered with debris. But there was a point of interest. The buildings I could see through my window were stuccoed white, a browned-yellow, and salmon; but in late afternoon, the white-stuccoed building appeared to be a pale, pea green, as did the walls of my room. The room itself was about the size of my college dorm room, or at least my half of the dorm room. In fact, there was not enough room to open my suitcase unless I laid it on the bed.

The bathroom was also interesting. There were faucets all over the place. Two were at a convenient height for foot washing. The fixed show-erhead was located on the back wall and aimed toward the middle of the room, so that it hit both sink and toilet when I turned it on. There was no defined boundary for the shower; in fact, the shower and the bathroom were one in the same, and the water drained into an opening in the floor beyond the sink. The pipes from the sink went into the wall, but spit the water out again from another pipe that protruded from the wall, so it splashed into the same hole as shower run-off. There was a huge bucket under the shower. At first I wasn't sure whether I was supposed to catch the shower water in the bucket or let it fall onto the stone floor. I opted for the latter, since I'd have had to dump the bucket into the floor drain anyway. I'm sure I missed a nuance, but it worked.

The best part of the bathroom was that clean towels were provided, which was not the case at Monica House. To bathe at Monica House, I'd have had to face the menacing market again and buy linens. For that reason alone, the Circular was worth the slightly higher price. However, I learned one important lesson: to make sure the lid on my toilet was closed before flushing, because it swirled the water around the bowl so hard when it flushed that it splashed onto the floor, and one day it began to spit black particles of unknown origin. Thank God for my antiseptic wipes—"Ideal for cleaning toilet seats, hand cleaning, etc." the package read.

I was so intrigued by all the knobs and faucets that I took photos of the bathroom, my first photos of the trip. Among the reasons I hadn't taken any pictures of the many interesting sights was that I didn't feel safe taking photos on the street, looking like a tourist who was not on guard.

By morning my throat hurt like a sonofabitch. The pain was mainly on the right side, with a patch of pain on the left soft palate. I felt feverish but didn't have a thermometer, and the light in my bathroom was too weak to allow me to examine my throat in the mirror. I decided to take a day or two off. I didn't want to add to the patients' suffering by giving them my disease.

I took my second dose of azithromycin. I expected to see a turn-around within 24 hours and didn't know what I would do if that didn't happen. Seated in the restaurant of the Circular, I took the antibiotic with "Mohun's Gold Coin" apple juice, "clarified and sweetened with sugar," along with my hot tea with sugar and milk, toast, and a cheese omelet. I enjoyed the toast at the hotel, which seemed like it was made from bakery bread rather than from something that was mass-produced.

The waiters were amused that I ate spicy food, like the Indians. I kept explaining that I come from Texas where the Mexican food is quite spicy, but they didn't believe that there could be food as spicy as theirs. Every once in a while, I could tell they'd thrown in some extra peppers to test me—especially when I saw the expectant looks on their faces—but I'm a stubborn ole gal, and I ate every bite. All in all, I have to say that the food was wonderful in Kolkata, despite the inherent risks of hepatitis A that come with uncooked vegetables washed in sewage-contaminated water.

Nonetheless, in the Circular I felt safe, and the food was lovely. One of my favorite meals was *alu chat* and Tandoori chicken. *Alu chat* is a delightful boiled potato dish with lemon, sliced fresh chilies, and parsley. The *tandoori* chicken is heavily spiced and baked in a clay oven. The hotel served it with a small side salad of julienne raw beets, onions, and cucumbers with lemon. Topped off by a cup of tea, the meal was perfect. In the heat, I often found it more pleasant to eat ice cream at the start of the meal. This let me cool down before I ordered. I love being middle-aged and able to do what I want.

I learned a lesson about how the Bengali table is set. On the restaurant table were two shakers that looked like salt and white pepper. However, when I put the white pepper on my food, it seemed no more spiced than before. Curious, I dumped some onto my hand and found it was flour. I've yet to learn why it was there.

The complexity of a country's cuisine reflects the age of its civilization. "Celebrate the New Year the Foodie Way" was the headline for an article listing restaurants to patronize on the Bengali New Year's day. In 1690, when Job Charnack of the British East India Company settled in the swamp that was to become Kolkata, the Bengalis he found were mainly fishermen and hunters. Rice grew wild in the fertile marshlands around what is now Kolkata, and rice remains its principal crop today. The land also yielded a plethora of tropical fruits: bananas, coconuts, mangoes, jackfruit, and wood apples. The waters teemed with the fish and crustaceans that are the backbone of Bengali cuisine. There was such bounty in the region, and the Indians believed that food was sacred. Along with this came the belief that sharing food is a virtue and hoarding a sin.

Chili peppers, although a staple in modern Bengali food preparation, are not indigenous to the area and were an import from Central America by way of Sri Lanka. Today they are grown prolifically in local gardens and used in almost every dish except dessert. Also imported were the potato and tomato, which are featured so prominently in today's Bengali cuisine that one would never have guessed. Other popular imports that have become part of daily life are the onion-and-spice-laden Muslim foods, such as kabobs. One could find English, French, Dutch, Armenian, and Chinese influence, though these cuisines have remained more ethnically distinct. One thing that has become universal is *chai*—the mix of black tea, cardamom, ginger, cloves, cinnamon, milk, and honey that has become popular throughout the United States.

I was fascinated watching people eat. If utensils weren't used, food was eaten with the right hand, which must always be kept clean. Similar to the traditions in Arab countries, the left hand is used for dirty work, such as toileting, so there is a cultural prohibition against eating, touching others, or offering money with the left hand.

Food could be served on plates or in banana leaves, and it was common to find sweets in tiny boxes made of banana leaves. Street vendors sold drinks in tiny terracotta cups that looked like there should be seedlings in them. People tossed them all over the sidewalks and into the gutters when they were through with them.

The heat and humidity overburdened the air conditioning in the restaurant, and I was drenched during dinner. All I wanted to do was pay the check and go upstairs to lie under the fan. The lack of circulating air in the restaurant was far worse than the heat. I felt so sorry for the waiters, who said it had been terrible in the kitchen that day. It must have been daunting to work next to a stove in an un-air-conditioned room.

I'd seen food vendors who traveled around carrying portable heating units on their backs to keep the food they sold warm. I couldn't even imagine what it must be like to haul burning coals on my back in this heat. For example, one day I worked for hours taping labels on medications that had been donated. I came back the next day only to find the heat had melted the tape and most of the labels had fallen off in the boxes. If I ever come back to Kolkata, I'll bring an indelible felt-tipped pen for labeling.

On the way home from the relative opulence of Park Street a few days before, I passed row after row of hovels created from black rubber sheeting and boards. They must be as hot as hell at night, since that rubber would block a good bit of the breeze. Poverty seemed more glaring along Park Street, where there were shops that looked too expensive, even for me. Being a shop-'til-you-drop kind of gal and a longtime patron of Saks Fifth Avenue and Neiman Marcus, that's saying something. Ironically, after I left, Park Street was renamed "Mother Teresa Sarani." I wonder how she would have felt about that particular street bearing her name.

It was hard to conceive of how the street population survived the heat, especially since the water wasn't safe. It was contaminated not only by sewage, but also by arsenic. *The Hindustan Times* reported that arsenic-contaminated water was such a persistent problem in certain districts that the health department had maintained free treatment programs and five free beds in Kolkata's SSKM Hospital for arsenic patients since 1986. The news story said that the department had suddenly decided to rescind the program and the beds. The article demanded that the government either provide arsenic-free drinking water or restore a free medical treatment facility, since nearly four hundred thousand people had no access to water that did not contain arsenic.[28]

And there were more stories of potential health catastrophes. Under the heading "Choke-o-meter," *The Times of India* reported that the city was suffering from high heat and pollution.[29] *The Times of India* story "Heat stroke kills one as city reels under heat wave," told how a street hawker died after being in the sun for six hours. "It was the first heat stroke death of the summer. And the season is still young."[30] As if that weren't disturbing enough, a final story from *The Times of India*, "Water pollution gives rise to gastro cases," announced:

> Kolkata: Gastroenteritis cases are on the rise in the city due to contamination of drinking water. In Dum Dum, leakage in water pipes has led to a jaundice outbreak with nearly 100 people being taken ill.[31]

The text went on to state that in one neighborhood alone, twenty-five people had been taken ill in the last five days from drinking sewage-laced water.

In such conditions, it was not surprising that volunteers had fallen ill. The number of volunteers who had contracted intestinal ailments was growing, but I'd actually been lucky on that score. In the United States I was plagued with allergies year-round; in Kolkata, my nose did not run.

I spoke with a volunteer from Tokyo who had been in the hospital for a week with coughing and bronchial pain. All she'd wanted was a TB test, but since she had insurance, she got the works until she finally demanded to be released.

Susan, an Australian nurse, was found unconscious and incontinent in her room, and had to be taken to the hospital. I was told she had "a liver infection," not further described. I am sure that will be a lifelong memento of Kolkata for her. Not coincidentally, *The Hindustan Times* reported that seven hundred fifty hepatitis cases had been reported in Dum Dum, the area around the airport, and there was a story about thirty persons falling ill from sewage-contaminated water at Raj Bhavan, the governor's magnificent residence. The problem was not restricted to the poorer areas.

Despite all this, I could see why Mother Teresa loved this place. I had begun to love it myself—all of it. Hospice nursing had taught me that beauty and ugliness are truly in the eyes of the beholder, and Mother Teresa saw beauty in the poor. She said, "The poor are the most precious gift of God to us—Jesus' hidden presence." Frankly, I think that how we regard the poor tells us a lot about ourselves on a most basic level.

WHAT WILL I REMEMBER?

My throat still hurt in the morning, and I knew I was infectious and should not get close to anyone. Sadly, it was Thursday, the volunteers' day off, and everyone was going to the leper colony in Titagarh where all the cloth used by the Missionaries of Charity is woven. I had wanted to see the colony, but the train would be packed and I'd have to sit close enough to transmit germs. The infectious disease nurse in me said no, even though this would be the last chance I'd have to visit the colony. I'd be going back home before the volunteers were scheduled to go again, I had no intention of taking a train trip out of the city by myself. Short bus and cab rides had been adventure enough.

By mid-morning, however, I felt anxious sitting around my hotel room. I kept telling myself that, sick or not, I'd regret missing a tourist day and, if I walked around by myself, I wouldn't have to get close enough to endanger others. Another motivation was that I was tired of reading medical textbooks and craved more understanding of India. I decided to walk to the Oxford Bookstore—that way I could see the sights along the way and buy something to read in the evening.

As I walked down Park Street to the bookstore, I noticed a distinct change from the places I usually frequented. Park Street, one of the wealthy shopping areas, was home to upscale sari stores and trendy cafes. Yet, despite the opulence, razor blades were strewn about the sidewalk, because men bathed and shaved there while shoppers picked their way around them without even looking down.

Where there is wealth in Kolkata, it is wealth beyond my understanding. Such wealth means more than money, it means tremendous social and political power that makes it possible to step around beggars and not consider helping. On the other hand, there is also poverty and cruelty—the kind that is found in regions that have only the very rich and the very poor. I'd seen similar situations in the Caribbean and desperately poor areas of Mexico, and read of it in Africa and Brazil. All Americans have seen films of children in famine-ridden and war-swept nations who suffer from Kwashiorkor—the kind of malnutrition that makes the belly swell and turns the hair a lighter-than-normal color. In the end, these children become too weak and complacent to raise their hands to chase the flies from their eyes. And, while the United States and other nations pump in food and supplies, it often does not reach the needy because corrupt governments care nothing for their people and do not distribute it. There was a bit of this in Kolkata, but rather than comparing Kolkata to the United States, I tried to think of it as another time, another place. It was a place that would prefer to change the West rather than be changed, so the more homogeneous distribution of wealth, orderly behavior, and abundant social services of the West will not come quickly to Kolkata, if at all. My decision has been to love it for what it is, not for what could be made of it. India will make her way on her terms. It is her choice, and that's how it should be, after all.

By and large, America's wealth far exceeds its needs, but diminishing America's wealth will not, in and of itself, ease the poverty of other lands. The wealthy in the destitute nations find ways to grab large-scale aid before it reaches those in need. I'm convinced that Mother Teresa's way is the best: provide pockets of hope to the poor by serving them, not by throwing money and consumables at them.

Along my route to the bookstore, I window-shopped at Park Street's exclusive shops, which displayed the saris of fantasies and fairly tales. Indeed, Indian fabrics were a special treat for the eye, and window displays featured silks of every color imaginable with embroidery, sparkling mirrors, beads, and sequins arranged in art of endless possibilities. The materials ranged from unadorned cotton to lavish silk brocades, and the prices for the better pieces exceeded what some on the street could make in a lifetime. Also, producing this splendor had an ugly side. The weavers who painstakingly created this beauty worked in sweatshop conditions and got slave wages, reminding me that there seems to be no in-between in this wondrously magical, horrible place.

I don't know if it's the cop or the nurse in me, but I very much enjoy people watching, and the sidewalks of Kolkata offer a rich environment for that. Many of the ladies carried umbrellas, and it struck me as ironic that the white women in the United States all want to get tan, while the women of India want to be pale. Fashion advertisements were full of products to keep the sun's rays from tanning the skin. The ads were not in English, so I wasn't sure exactly what was being said, but they inevitably depicted a man admiring an Indian woman's light skin. One ad portrayed a woman shunning an umbrella as if she could stay pale without it. Her secret was the skin lotion they were advertising.

The older I get, the more I recognize what evil the fashion industry imposes on women by telling them they're not good enough as they are. Indian culture promotes this ideal as well. The Sunday *Hindustan Times* ran a matrimonial section where people advertised for spouses. Most ads for wives specified fair skin. I don't understand it, because the darker skin against the coal black hair is stunning. Also, Indian women could wear almost any color against their skin. As a pale-skinned woman, my choices were restricted. Yellow makes me look jaundiced, as does lime. Blood reds and bright colors are great, but I envy the darker skin tones that seem to glow against any hue.

Between Park Street's sari stores and the bookstore was a police station. Kolkata police looked like soldiers dressed in sharp brown uniforms. They carried rifles instead of side arms. Even in this there was incongruity: some of the police weapons appeared to be of wood and were not automatics. When they stood post at police stations, their rifles had bayonets affixed and the officers barricaded themselves behind piles of sandbags. I scurried past the stations as quickly as possible, knowing that terrorist bombs were a fairly common occurrence in India. Police stations, bus stops, and markets were known targets. In fact, the national elections were proving to be so violent that the military had been called in to protect polling places. The newspapers were full of the various candidates and parties, as well as the dangers inherent in running for office in India, where there was a rich history of political passion and assassination. Incumbent Mohammad Shahabuddin was running for office from his Bihar jail cell, while awaiting trial for the kidnapping and possible murder of a rival party activist. Shahabuddin was also charged in more than thirty other cases that ranged from murder to bank robbery to kidnapping.

Even the school buses looked military. One passed while I was attempting to cross the street. It was more like an army transport than a school bus, because it was olive drab with wooden benches three across. There was black string netting on the windows. However, it said "school bus" in big letters across the front. Still, the robustly healthy, uniformed children who poured from the schools along Park Street looked like Catholic school children anywhere in the United States. The boys had ties and the girls wore little jumpers. All had nice shoes, which was in sharp contrast to the children on most of the streets I'd seen.

After a half-hour stroll, I arrived at the Oxford Bookstore, a well appointed, well stocked, and best of all, air-conditioned shop. Within minutes, I'd loaded up both arms with books I wanted to buy and had climbed the stairs to the little cafe with its excellent view of the street and the people below.

As I sat in the climate-controlled comfort of the Oxford's cafe, sipping *chai* and nibbling a chocolate sweet, I felt that I was being given a special privilege. It was curious how much more I was enjoying so many of the things I simply didn't notice in the United States. I guess it takes contrasts to make us see what we really have, and Kolkata was certainly a contrast to my usual lifestyle. Having said that, I must add that Kolkata isn't bad when compared to the United States; it is just different. I think the Western view of Kolkata can be colored by what we want to see in ourselves. Many can only see the Kolkata described in *City of Joy*. There is some of that, but that is not a full picture. All in all, I'd say that too much is made of the differences between India and the West. Oh, there are differences all right—big ones. But I was over-prepared to be shocked. I expected bad smells everywhere, but other than petroleum and the occasional open latrine, there were none. The cab drivers and taxis continued to exceed my worst expectations, and there were plenty of people living on the street, but they were treated with a much greater live-and-let-live attitude than in cities such as Washington, D.C. Of course, there are shelters in D.C., and the street people can get food at the shelters. Also, we rarely see children begging in the United States.

Children begging on the streets were an all-too-common sight in India. Most of the children who begged for a living in Kolkata didn't seem to be starving, and it came across as a bit of a racket. For example, more than once I'd watched children finish begging on a bus, then disembark and hand their money to well-dressed men who were waiting to snatch it from their hands. These guys were basically their pimps.

The young beggar boys jumped on the buses and performed songs. Some had surprisingly strong and beautiful voices. Others carried elongated, smooth, flat stones that they placed between the middle fingers of one hand and rapped against each other like percussion instruments. It made a sound similar to castanets. Every one of these boys assumed the same begging stance. They held out one hand, palm up, and then wagged their heads back and forth, tilting from side to side. The whiny voice they put on did not ring true. Older boys got aggressive. Sometimes they grabbed onto people and refused to let go.

Mark, one of the American doctors who came to the House for Sick and Dying Destitutes with Liz, did not look down when a boy was begging on the bus we rode to *Kalighat*. After a few moments of trying to catch Mark's attention, the child pinched him in the chest. When Mark recounted this event with obvious embarrassment, he termed it "a strange gesture." We were roaring with laughter when he said that he feared what might come next, so he'd given the boy some money.

Mothers, too, could be con artists. In one scam, a mother with baby on hip asks tourists to buy powdered milk for the baby. Once she has convinced the tourists to do this, she leads them to a store to buy it. When the milk is in hand, the mother thanks the tourists profusely, then returns to the store and resells it to the storeowner, who keeps a commission. To ensure that the baby gets the milk, you have to open the package before you hand it over to the mother. Many times I watched the sisters snip the corner off a sealed bag of powdered milk before giving it to a mother at free clinics. How glad I am not to have the lifetime experience that would lead me to understand what would drive a mother to sell the food her baby needed.

There's no doubt that Kolkata is a city with great beauty and harsh realities, with wealth beyond imagination and abject poverty. The architecture is intricate and the literary tradition rich, but the city structures suffer from the charcoal-grayness of pollution that afflicts many formerly communist cities of Central Europe. Still, beneath the haze of soot are the artistic creations that earned Kolkata the name "City of Palaces" when it was the secondary capital of the British Empire.

Poverty, pollution, sand, and insane traffic are its greatest negatives, but there is much more to the city than these drawbacks. It is a city where both rich and poor find ways to live. Kolkata encompasses four hundred twenty six square kilometers with a population of about thirteen and two tenths million people. That means that the population density is just under thirty one thousand per square kilometer. However, Kolkata's inflation does not approach that of Mumbai or Bangalore, so the poorest of the poor scrape by. In fact, though I had seen quite a few people sleeping on the sidewalk—either alone or in small beggar communities—I had yet to see anyone dying of starvation on the street, as had been my expectation before I arrived.

The spiciness of the air and the acrid petroleum pollution are the olfactory memories I'd take with me. The splash of gold, red, and fuchsia flowers, contrasted with the black-gray grime of sand and pollution that pockmarks the brick structures and settles in your lungs, were the colors that are locked in my mind. As a matter of fact, my plastic scrub watch had become increasingly browner. It had been a light jade in color when I bought it, but after a couple of weeks in Kolkata, there were only a few strips that retained the original hue. Since I was certain that the color change was due to pollution, I was afraid to find out what my lung tissue might look like and how long it would take it to repair itself.

The people who lived on the street worked constantly to keep themselves clean. They got covered in the same muck that assaulted the buildings, but they washed all day long. The water they used sometimes appeared no cleaner than the dirt that it removed from their bodies, but they persistently drenched themselves and their clothing nonetheless.

I spent the bulk of my time in poorer areas, but there were nicer places. Kolkata had an air-conditioned subway. Though it was an efficient and clean transportation system, it was a little disconcerting to find that the subway—the air-conditioned pride of Kolkata—had buckets of sand hanging from stands around the concourse for fire emergencies. Photographs were not allowed in the subway, due to fear of terrorist attacks. Not realizing this, I took my camera out to capture a shot of the sand buckets and people started shouting and pointing at me. I put it away without snapping any shots.

A Filipino friend broke my reverie at the cafe and said the heat had spoiled the visit to the leper colony at Titagarh. He said the train had been sweltering and overfilled. I felt a little better about not going, since I would never have made it through the trip without passing out, and I would have infected other volunteers. For their sakes, I knew I should stay home yet another day, but I was feeling guilty—the perpetually nursing quandary: responsibility vs. being responsible.

As I started to the hotel, I noticed that my arms were burning in the sun. At that point I remembered how antibiotics could make your skin photosensitive, but it was a bit too late to apply lotion. I knew I'd have to cover up until I'd finished the series of azithromycin, which would not be inviting in the heat.

Along the path from the bookstore to the hotel was a cemetery. I wanted to wander through it but fear of a serious burn prevented me from doing it that day. Its rows of crosses still piqued my interest. It occurred to me that Hindus like to be cremated, so I surmised it was a historic burial ground from colonial days. From a distance, it appeared to be wellmaintained, and I vowed that I would explore it before I left Kolkata.

I love history and every street corner of Kolkata exuded it. In my experience, there seemed to be something for everyone in Kolkata, but the challenges were not always brought on by Kolkatans or their culture. Carolyn, the Australian emergency department nurse, lived in Sudder Street, which was quite popular with tourists and Missionaries of Charity volunteers. Some of the places were nice, but—to Caroline's dismay—her hotel housed a bunch of dope smokers who stayed up all night getting high and listening to a French swami rave into the wee hours of the morning. These sessions were so loud that she could hear their conversations in her room. Though the swami was practically nonsensical, his followers did not care. They just inhaled and hung on his every word. It sounded like a 1960s quest for enlightenment revisited. They would have been better enlightened working for the poor and sick.

All in all, Carolyn hadn't had the best of luck on this trip. Her woes started when she flew to Tibet with a tour group. Tibet being so close, it seemed a shame to miss it, but there was fighting in Kathmandu, so her group was stopped at the border and lodged in a hotel for the night. In the middle of the night, a man with an automatic shoulder weapon burst into her room and ordered her out. Gunmen were rounding up foreigners. The tour guide bribed their way out and negotiated a propeller plane. Unfortunately, Carolyn was afraid of flying in small aircraft and the prop plane belonged to an obscure local airline, so there was no guarantee it had been maintained. She was crying by the time the plane left the ground. A masseuse happened to be in the seat behind her and massaged her shoulders all the way to India in an attempt to calm her—another demonstration of the contrasts in cruelty and kindness that mark day-to-day life in that part of the world.

Mother Teresa understood best what unites all of us: the human spirit of the individual. On my way home from the Oxford Bookstore, I lugged armfuls of books I'd bought to help me remember and sort out the onslaught of what I'd seen in India. I hoped the books would provide context for the many things that compelled thought and, so far, defied satisfying explanation. But words alone could not suffice, so I'd bought plenty of picture books to show family and friends. Still, the places depicted in these books didn't capture it—they were too clean, as if they had shooed away the people and swept up the sand and rubbish before the photos were taken.

Lost in thought, I contemplated why I hadn't taken pictures of my own. It was not that there weren't a million photographic subjects to explore. At first, it had been safety concerns—not making myself a mark because I looked like a tourist. But in the end, I just didn't see these people and places as a sideshow. People lived on the street, and photographing them seemed akin to invading their homes.

The essence of Kolkata was there on the sidewalks and streets—the good and the bad. Bad things had happened because I was too trusting, but every now and then, something happened that reinforced my faith. For example, that day, on the way home from the bookstore, I fell and rolled out into the middle of the street. I was carrying at least twenty books, some of substantial size, which weighed me down, and—let's face it—I'm a klutz. I've capsized in downtown D.C. as well, but it wasn't quite as scary. Kolkata's traffic hurled pell-mell about the streets, bent only on jockeying for position. "Aggressive driving" was a weak descriptor. In D.C., cars more often fuse together into long, slow-moving rush-hour pythons, and D.C. drivers know they'll be found at fault if they hit pedestrians, so you have a prayer of escaping death.

Anyway, as I rolled into the street, three men saw me fall. They shouted at the oncoming drivers to stop, shielding me with their own bodies, then helped me up. I got filthy and suffered a few abrasions on my hands and right knee, but nothing was broken. What these men did demonstrated why I cling to Tagore's words: "I shall not commit the grievous sin of losing faith in Man."

Which brings me to Mother Teresa's. If I had to describe one memory of the House for Sick and Dying Destitutes, it would not be the maggot-filled wounds, the patients scarred from whippings, tuberculosis, leishmaniasis, mental illness, or the women who had been burned by their husbands. The overriding image I carry is one of smiling patients—people who never dreamt they'd be treated as sentient beings as long as they walked this earth. But they were at Mother Teresa's, and the followers of this simple woman and her God provide hope without imposing religion. They serve for the privilege of serving alone. They do not preach or ask for thanks. They believe that their work is a vision of God to those who would see, and that is enough.

DISPENSARY IN THE COUNTRYSIDE

Sister Lumen arranged for Carolyn and me to work in the dispensary, which is located in a rural area outside the city. We rode in the Missionaries of Charity's truck with medicines packed in every corner, even under the wooden benches we were sitting on in the back. We prayed the rosary and sang all the way to the dispensary.

Although I still didn't know the rosary, I used the time for contemplation, and the singing was wonderful. In fact, the sisters' singing continued to charm me. It was the sweetest, most innocent sound I'd ever heard. Many of the novices were just out of school, and on the way home they were playing little tricks on each other. One tied another's apron strings to a bench. As they giggled over these pranks, I felt free from worry. Their ability to focus on small joys was inspiring and the sadness of the world around us didn't seem so staggering. When I was with them, I could focus on my blessings because I was so happy.

It was quite an adventure driving through the countryside, and a major change in scenery. The rural areas felt the effects of drought and famine more acutely, because when the crops failed, the people starved. The bucolic terrain tricked the eye into perceiving that people were better off, since they weren't piled on top of each other as in the city. Yet an indication of the great need was the numbers of women, children, and men who lined the courtyard as we entered the white stucco church cum clinic complex, which was guarded by a statue of Mary that was fashioned after the one at Lourdes.

At the dispensary, it was hard to walk the line between helping people and enabling negative behavior. Some of the people who came to us shopped around the clinical areas we set up. When they didn't get what they wanted from one nurse, they went to another across the courtyard.

We triaged people into three areas. One was set up for children, one for adults, and one for people who only needed pharmaceutical products. Some patients went to doctors' stands and were given chits for drugs, then came to the pharmacy to receive them. Others had orders from the hospital or were regular customers who needed refills on already-prescribed medications and were directed to the pharmacy stand. Still others avoided triage and came directly to the pharmacy, where we diagnosed and treated minor complaints that didn't warrant the doctor's time or referred those who looked sicker to the physician.

I examined a young girl with a tumor on the lower left quadrant of her abdomen. The tumor looked like a bunch of flesh-colored grapes, due to the multiple spherical formations. It was like some I'd seen in terminal patients with stage-four colon cancer. The doctor later confirmed that I was probably right. The mass protruded from an old surgical scar, but the family didn't seem to understand that we did not have anything that would make it go away. There was, however, one thing I could offer: Metrogel, which I like to use in wound dressing when *Pseudomonas* is suspected but also works well on tumor odor. Luckily, I had bought a tube the day before, intending to use it on patients at *Kalighat*, and had forgotten to take it out of my nursing apron.

When we first arrived at the clinic, Carolyn spotted a baby with cerebral palsy. As it turned out, what looked like a several-months-old, undernourished infant was a two-year-old boy. Carolyn asked to hold him, and as soon as she took him in her arms, he urinated in her face. Ah, the pleasures of nursing. Then, to our shock, the mother tried to get Carolyn to keep the child. Such desperation is beyond the comprehension of most of us in the West.

American society, of course, has elements that are equally hard to understand. While we were loading the truck for the trip, Sister Lumen and I talked about American society and mores. The sisters are shocked by the news stories that filled international papers about the U.S. We are a violent society—not that there is no violence in India, there is plenty—but it is harder for me to understand violence when we have so much to make us happy. Our children kill each other for wearing the wrong colors or to steal expensive tennis shoes, and illegal drugs, our greatest scourge, are a plague of self-centeredness. Still, even the poorest of U.S. families do not maim their children to heighten their appeal for begging, and everyone can get access to social services, even if it is a highly inconvenient and inconsistent system. Somehow violence in the context of U.S. society just seems more purposeful and pointless.

Sister Lumen, who had been a nurse in Baltimore, told me about a woman who sent her young boy out to run drugs, thinking that he wouldn't end up in jail because he had not yet reached his teens. The mother was herself an addict, and when the boy brought home an evening's drugs and money, which he was to give to the dealer, she pilfered from it, leaving the child unable to deliver what the dealer expected from him. Eventually, the dealer shot the boy in the head and he ended up in the hospital where Sister Lumen worked. Among other things, the boy was blinded. Though it was not expected, he regained his sight, which, considering the extent of his injuries, was a miracle.

Over his lengthy recovery, he became the nurses' favorite. The hospital attempted to have him removed from the home, but to no avail. When he was released from the hospital, he returned to running drugs; and when his mother needed to get high, she stole from him. In the end, the drug dealer killed him.

I also learned in that conversation that the sisters who normally attended dispensary—mostly nurses and one doctor—had spent a day at *Kalighat* while I was ill. While there, they examined Kavita's burns and realized that nothing they could do would cure her. Her lungs were fluid-filled—a signal that the dying process had begun. They removed Kavita's IVs because they would contribute to the wetness in her lungs, plus they were serving no curative or comfort purpose. We agreed it was time to let God handle the situation, and I felt relieved because I knew that Kavita would soon be out of pain.

When we returned to the dispensary's courtyard, the sick and needy crowded the grounds. While waiting for medications, a wizened, elderly woman fainted on the porch. As there was no one with her, Carolyn and I carried her out to a tree and placed her in the shade. She could not have weighed more than ninety pounds. I had no idea how old she was, because life was so much harder in India and apparent age was deceptive.

Once we'd revived her, we gave her some water. It was sad to see this shell of a woman lying there so listlessly and to know that this was the way of life in the Indian countryside. The temperature on Bengali New Year's had topped thirty-eight degrees Celsius, which is one hundred point four degrees Fahrenheit. The weather report predicted no break in the heat for the month of April, and people can't function long without water. What luxury we live in to be able to drink water whenever we want—and safe water, at that.

As we were leaving dispensary, I gave a pen to a teenage girl who was a deaf-mute. I saw how she was eyeing my apron pocket from which one of the many Bic pens I'd brought from the U.S. peeked out. I had a whole package at the hotel, so I gave it to her without considering that there might be consequences. The impulse to give was hard to resist sometimes, but this time it turned out to be a big mistake, albeit borne of good intentions. I saw my error almost as soon as I gave the gift, when my casual act almost started a stampede.

Two German doctors also tossed pens to the crowd when they saw that others wanted them. I was disgusted to see the men grab more for themselves, elbowing out the women and children. Earlier, I had given my Miraculous Medal to a mother holding a baby, but then I was a little more clandestine and no one else noticed, except that a passing sister smiled as the woman kissed the medal then used it to make the sign of the cross over the baby's face and pressed it to the child's forehead.

As I watched these people grappling for what we would consider disposable trinkets in the West, I was reminded of a news article I read in the *Times of India*. More than twenty women had died because someone was handing out free saris for the New Year. So many women were vying for them that those who fell underfoot were crushed to death.

On the ride home, we ate some protein biscuits as we sat on wooden benches in the back of the truck. The Dutch Army had pledged to provide these biscuits to all of Mother Teresa's facilities "for life." Slightly sweet, they tasted vaguely like *petit beurre* cookies, but each has the protein content of two eggs.

We drove back to *Shishu Bhavan*, where I watched the sisters turn away a woman and child brought in by a British teenager. If I were new in Kolkata, I'd have been appalled, but the woman was a regular who used the child to scam tourists.

The child did not appear to be ill, so the sisters explained to the teen that they were familiar with the woman and she knew the hours of operation. They told him the woman could bring her child back in two hours or go directly to a hospital that would treat the child without charge. The teen couldn't see that the woman was deceiving him, nor would he understand that the two hours before the facility opened again was the time for the sisters' prayer and for them to perform the maintenance that made the place livable. I felt sorry for the sisters, because it was a difficult situation. But I knew they were right, especially after my experience of trying to give the young woman a pen at dispensary.

After dinner, I encountered an elderly woman lying alone on the sidewalk near the Circular Hotel. She was dressed in rags and reached out to me with bony, claw-like hands. Touched, I gave her a ten-rupee bill, which would have been enough to buy some food, but she wanted more. She railed at me, as if offended, as if I owed her more.

I'd had similar experiences when I worked in Washington, D.C. and also when I volunteered at Martha's Table, a wonderful charity in D.C. that offers a variety of programs, one of which is food vans. We'd ride to specific stops in the vans and pass out soup and sandwiches to anyone who came. Each person received two kinds of sandwiches: one meat and one peanut butter and jelly. Often the people took the meat sandwiches and threw the peanut butter and jelly on the ground, angry that they couldn't get two meat sandwiches. I was told that some actually sold the sandwiches. Again, I didn't understand, but I was glad I hadn't learned the tough lessons that would have led me to understand.

As I readied myself for bed, I turned the air conditioning on full blast to cool the room as quickly as possible. The air and fan were too much in combination, so once the room cooled down, I turned the fan off and climbed into bed. As I lay on the bed, the blades of the fan revealed themselves slowly, then more clearly, like life in Kolkata.

QUANDARIES

When I arrived at *Kalighat* the next morning, I found Kavita still hanging on. Although I couldn't understand her language, she appeared to be delirious, rolling her head from side to side, grinding her teeth, and emitting growling sounds. The relaxant diazepam had not eased the tooth grinding. Hanging from her inner elbows were IVs. Thomasina had restarted them and wrapped an enormous amount of gauze on the arms so that they would be difficult to remove. From a nursing standpoint, the gauze was a critical problem because it kept us from checking whether the IV insertion sites were healthy and not damaged by needles that had slipped out of place. When needles dislodge from the veins, fluid goes into surrounding tissues. This causes swelling and the fluid does the patient no good. Also, if the site becomes infected, it is possible for the blood to carry it around the body and cause a lethal systemic infection. All in all, hiding an IV site from view was a poor choice, especially because the proper IV tapes were available at *Kalighat*.

Thomasina thought she was saving Kavita, but the IV would only keep the volume in Kavita's circulatory system high enough to maintain her blood pressure and delay shock for a few excruciating hours. As it turned out, Kavita would die the following day.

The hospice nurse in me says that if I can't make it better, let nature take its course. At hospice, we don't do anything that is intended to hasten death, but we don't extend life either, unless we can offer comfort and quality of life in the bargain. To me, unless a patient requests it, extending life without comfort is medical torture. I believe what it says in the Bible: there is a time to live and a time to die.

It's odd that in church we Christians pray for the day we'll be in heaven, yet when that time approaches, we all fight it as if it were evil. I think that part of the reason for this, at least in U.S., is that we no longer see the dying process as natural. When the norm was for extended families to live together, people participated in the care of their sick and aging families. They knew what death looked like; what it is and what it is not. The sick were not hidden away in sterile hospitals, and while people survive much better due to the availability of modern medicine, death no longer seems a natural ending. It is viewed as a medical failure and we sue doctors who can't stop it. In the process, we have lost the perspective that death has a purpose. It is natural and can be a relief. For those who reach the point where there is no cure and do not want to live out their numbered days undergoing treatments that will steal their strength and cost them precious moments of living that they could share with loved ones, there is hospice. I wish Thomasina had known more of this. I think she saw life as a win or lose proposition, and if Kavita died, there was only loss. Death heals many things and in that, it can be a victory over life. Thinking about Kavita's death does not make me nearly as sad as thinking about what her life must have been like. As I see it, God healed her through the gift of death.

My concern turned to Bina, a young woman who appeared to be about twenty years old, with wavy black, shoulder-length hair against a smooth, ebony complexion. This beautiful girl at the threshold of adulthood was in severe respiratory distress. Regretfully, I knew only basic treatments for respiratory distress, so I couldn't get too creative.

Her inhaler did nothing for her, and there was no nebulizer. There was also no morphine, which we use at hospice because it serves as both a bronchodilator and calming agent. Panic goes hand in glove with severe respiratory problems and creates a self-reinforcing cycle. The patient can't breathe, so he becomes anxious. Anxiety increases the patient's respiratory rate, making it even harder to breathe deeply enough to get sufficient oxygen, so the patient feels like he's suffocating, and fear increases.

I gave Bina injections of theophylline, which dilates bronchial passages, and diazepam when she was in crisis, then put her on the oldest oxygen tank I've ever seen. I set the flow at two liters, since I was told that she has chronic obstructive pulmonary disease (COPD), and COPD patients cannot tolerate higher doses of oxygen, because it actually makes them stop breathing.

I found a volunteer to sit with Bina, hoping it would ease her panic to know she was not alone. But Bina was not appreciably better when I left, and I was at a loss as to what else to try. There are no nurses on duty at night at *Kalighat*, since volunteers can only work during the day, so I prayed that she could hold on until I could research treatment strategies over the Internet.

Sadly, four doctors had convinced the sisters that Bina was faking it. The last one said that because of the excitement surrounding Easter and the Bengali New Year, Bina was trying to get attention. I could hardly hear breath sounds in the left lung, which indicated severe dysfunction. On top of that, she was wheezing in the "good" lung. I was enraged when I heard what those doctors had said, and I'm afraid I lectured Sister Georgina, who listened quietly as I told her that Bina had the classic signs of respiratory distress: Her lungs sounded terrible; she was panicked, panting, and sweating profusely. She held her upper body in the tripod position, arms resting on widespread elbows to open up the lung fields.

The look on Sister Georgina's face told me that she trusted my opinion, and the sadness in her eyes reminded me that she was not a nurse. All she had done was rely upon the doctors, the same ones she would have to rely upon after I left. I didn't blame her, but I kept thinking how I'd like to get my hands on these judgmental incompetents who said that Bina was just trying to get attention. I had some sharp words to share with them, despite Mother Teresa's warning that "Words which do not give the light of Christ increase the darkness."

Anjali, on the other hand, was nearly healed. She sat on her cot and played like a young child, and she talked and laughed to herself in a way that made me wonder whether she was mentally competent. Yet she was the one bright spot as I worried over Bina. I was sitting on Anjali's bed while Bina's breathing was out of control. I, too, was feeling the panic because nothing I did seemed to work and I was afraid that Bina would die then and there. Frustrated and on the verge of tears, I felt Anjali's hand slip through my arm. As I talked to Bina, Anjali patted my arm in the same way that I had patted hers the first day we met.

Contrasts like these redeemed the worst moments at *Kalighat*, and miraculous kindness balanced moments of despair; but that day brought more quandaries. Malti, a doll-like young woman with delicate, diminutive features that matched her body, was pointing to her abdomen and making a face like she was in pain. She spoke only Marithi, a tribal language from an area near Mumbai, and did not understand Hindi. Only one sister, who wasn't a nurse and was not always at *Kalighat*, could communicate with Malti, so she was left with pointing at her abdomen and making faces.

Diagnosing the female abdomen without being able to ask questions is problematic because our reproductive organs can reflect pain all over the place. For example, ovaries can hurt in the lower back and menstrual cramps can feel just like intestinal cramps. I couldn't feel any abnormalities in her organs and she wasn't bleeding, so I had to go with what I'd been told: that she had digestive problems. During the exam, she pointed to the epigastric area, which is the upper abdomen, just below the split of the ribs, and made a face that indicated pain. This was too high to be her intestines, and it was right in the center of the upper abdomen, so stomach pain was a reasonable conclusion.

Since there were no antacids or other stomach-protectors prescribed for her at the time, I added a chewable antacid before meals. We'd try that for a day or so and see whether it offered any relief. If so, we'd try something like famotedine—also known as Pepsid—a couple of times a day as a longer term prescription to help control the situation before it caused pain.

Kshama posed a much more difficult problem. She was a skeletal, psychotic woman with enormous haunting eyes reminiscent of Edvard Munch's 1893 painting *The Scream*. She had multiple wounds, horrible infection, and the skin was coming off her hand and arm as if removing a glove. She had developed another problem: the more or less intact areas of skin on her arm were macerating. I wasn't sure whether the cause was the exudate (wound drainage) or the disease process.

Due to her psychosis, she was constantly waving her arms around and dragging them along the floor. She tore at her bandages, never leaving them intact from shift to shift, so it was difficult to determine the amount her wounds drained in a 24-hour period.

Sometimes we used an iodine cream on Kshama's wounds before dressing it. This is not my first choice for wound care, for more than one reason—the most important being that iodine can inhibit new tissue growth. It also discolors anything it touches, so it distorts the color of exudate and dressings, rendering virtually useless one sign that I would use to evaluate infection. In the United States, we wash with normal saline, apply something to keep the wound bed moist—most often a saline gel, because it imitates the fluid that naturally exists in a healing wound bed—then rely upon antibiotics to treat the infection from the inside. But *Kalighat* isn't in the United States; it's in India, where iodine is antiseptic, cheap, and readily available, and saline gel is not.

Portions of Kshama's skin had detached between the wounds, and it had lifted up (a rather sickening sight to see) when Liz had sharps-debrided the necrotic tissue the other day. However, Kshama had shown absolutely no sign of pain during the procedure, so the nerves must have been dead in that area.

Because of her psychosis, it usually took two people to clean and bandage Kshama's wounds, and I was assisting Susan, the Australian nurse who had recently returned from the hospital after being treated for hepatitis. As she debrided Kshama's prurient wounds, I sat on the edge of a cot belonging to a woman named Mamta and held Kshama's arm still. Until then I'd had no interaction with Mamta, except to give her vitamins and chat. "Chat" isn't exactly the word, since she only spoke Bengali and I didn't understand a word of it. We smiled and nodded while I spoke English and she responded in Bengali. Without understanding her words, I could tell whether she needed anything because she pantomimed what she wanted.

Mamta watched us with interest as we worked on Kshama's arm. Kshama sat still but was raving about something and waving her free arm. She separated each word she spoke, as if proclaiming something of great importance, and her eyelids widened until the orbs bulged out. My overall impression was that she was delivering a warning about some sort of cosmic evil, because she kept pointing skyward and her face and tone of voice were foreboding.

Mamta paid Kshama little heed. In fact, she giggled as Kshama cursed and threatened. Mamta was interested in the medical procedure and kept shifting around to get a better view. At intervals she interjected comments and nodded approval.

When we finished bandaging Kshama, I stripped off my gloves. Mamta took my left hand, turned it over, and compared my palm to hers. She studied the palms for a while, then pointed to my head line and drew her forehead to it. She started speaking rapidly and pointing to a picture of the Holy Family, which was hanging on the wall. I couldn't tell whether she was blessing me or perhaps wanted a blessing, but she seemed happy.

In the past, she had touched my feet then touched her forehead. I always smiled and sometimes we touched forehead to forehead, but I was uncomfortable with imitating too much because I had no idea what it all meant.

The young man with pneumonia, whom I feared I'd killed when I pushed diazepam into his IV, was healing and now regarded me as his savior. Mark, one of the doctors from the United States who had spent the day with us, had decided what medication to give the man. If one of us were a savior, it was Mark. Nevertheless, since I administered the medication, the man thought I had saved him. Each time he saw me, he put his hands together and, with a beseeching look, touched his hands to his forehead, then his lips. I did the same. Without an interpreter I couldn't explain my role in all this, and I was just glad he was still alive.

Anuradha, the young woman with the paralyzed legs and urinary retention, convinced those on the cots around her that they must listen to me because I would cure them. This was a heavier burden than I could bear. I kept emphasizing that I'm a nurse and not a doctor, but she believed what she believed. Since having faith in your healthcare worker has a placebo effect, I should have just gone with the flow, but I would have never allowed this belief to stand if I were nursing in the United States, and I felt very uncomfortable with it in Kolkata.

My lack of saintly powers was demonstrated in the case of Jaya, the woman with the grossly swollen lower extremities and multiple leg wounds. Her family found out that she was at *Kalighat* and came to see her. They told us she had elephantiasis, so we could get the right medicine. We'd had no idea of that diagnosis and had only been treating her wounds, not the source of the problem. Up to that point, elephantiasis hadn't even entered my mind.

Elephantiasis is a condition that results from filariasis, a parasitic disease of the lymphatic system. Filariasis is caused by worms (*filariae*) that enter the body through mosquito bites. They live in the lymphatic system and release their eggs into the blood, which is where the mosquitoes pick them up. Filariasis is endemic in at least eighty countries, including some in South America and the Caribbean. Though it affects millions of people, it is rarely seen in the United States.

The *filariae* can cause a variety of problems because they clog up the lymphatic system so it can no longer conduct its immune system functions, leaving their victim open to infection. As they accumulate over the years, the adult worms amass in the lymphatic system so that it cannot work efficiently, and the lymphatic system can no longer drain proteins that leak from the blood vessels into tissue spaces known as the interstitium. The protein draws fluid into interstitial spaces and there is no place for it to go. This results in edema that is difficult to relieve. Due to the massive swelling and blockages, the bloated tissue becomes malnourished and susceptible to ulcerations that are difficult to heal. Elephantiasis is an advanced stage of lymphedema caused by filariasis. Medicine can kill the parasites and reduce the swelling to an extent, but the affected limbs will never return to their normal size.

While it is important to think through medical conditions such as Jaya's carefully for the patients' sake, sometimes concentrating on clinical data also helped me take my mind off worry and stress. I was still smarting over an incident that had occurred a couple of days previously. One of the major contributors—a wealthy, overfed Chinese woman, a member of Kolkata's large Chinese émigré community—yelled at me because I took a patient's picture after I'd finished bandaging her. I had the patient's permission to take the picture, but the Chinese woman didn't care. She had decided that no pictures should be taken. What is more, she had been standing in the middle of the women's ward, dripping jewelry and yelling at volunteers to do this and that, as if we were servants who needed direction. She, on the other hand, did not lift a finger for a patient.

The sisters were too nice to confront her, and in their presence, I didn't feel right about it either, but I was mad at myself for walking away. I wish I had at least said, "Don't talk to me that way." Instead, I took a break from patient care and washed dishes.

I should not have allowed myself to get grouchy at *Kalighat*, but the daily frustrations were getting to me. Mother Teresa emphasized not hiding your light under a bushel, letting people see your good work. I'm afraid the bushel slammed shut on me that day.

A READING ON LIFE IN KOLKATA

Indian newspaper stories were a consistent source of interest for me. No matter how much I thought I was beginning to understand life in India, when I picked up the news, I realized how little I understood.

Here's a disturbing sample from *The Telegraph Calcutta*, entitled "Death rules roost, brides keep off." It focused on a teacher, known only as "Sir," who could not find a bride in the village of Vidharba, which the article describes as being "full of dark tales and rancid smell." The village men complain that they cannot find wives in this town "where it is routine for women to hang themselves due to helplessness and poverty."

The reporter opined that "Sir" would never find a bride, even though girls as young as twelve have their virginity "sold" to the highest bidder at open fairs in parts of interior Vidharba. All this makes for a grim lifestyle that many women do not live to tell about. Just recently, a townswoman tried to hang herself from a beam in her hut. Though she survived death, villagers "are not sure she will survive the attempts being made by her husband to marry for the third time in search of a male child."[32]

There were other articles about suicides. One called "By Their Own Hand" said that worldwide suicide rates "are about three times higher for men than women." However, a group of researchers at the Christian Medical College in Vellore, India, published an article in *The Lancet* that said, "...in developing countries in Asia, suicide is far more common among young females." They attributed this to "lack of education, conflicts surrounding the issue of arranged marriages, love failures, dowries and things like that."[33]

In fact, many Indian women live in fear that their husbands will harm them to extort more dowry from their families. It is also well known that burning is a common way men rid themselves of unwanted wives, yet the police seem to take at face value that there are an inordinate number of clumsy women in India who sustain burns in "cooking accidents." Marriage can be perilous for women in this land where dowries are a life-long moneymaking scheme for the groom and his family. For example, *The Hindustan Times* reported the death of an eighteen-year-old girl. Neighbors called the police when they saw her in-laws trying to stuff her body into a car. The neighbors asked what was wrong and the in-laws said the girl had fallen ill and they were taking her to the hospital, but the neighbors could see that she was dead. They had become suspicious when the house, from which the sounds of arguments always came, had been unusually quiet for a couple of days. It was known that the family quarreled over the girl's dowry and that the girl's father had offered to take the girl back home, as he could pay no more. The police arrested the entire family, except the girl's husband, who got away. It appeared that the girl had been strangled.

The *Hindustan Times* ran yet another story called "No place at home if either parent dislikes your wife." It recounts a recent Kolkata High Court decision concerning an elderly man who brought a young mistress to live in his house and was trying to pass her off as his son's wife. Neither the son nor the elderly man's real wife was pleased about the situation. Judge Barin Ghosh's "landmark ruling" was that "A son and his wife have no right to stay at his parents' home if any one of the parents doesn't like either the son or his wife."[34]

In contrast, *The Hindustan Times* featured a classified section for high-tech jobs. Information technology schools often displayed photographs of women and girls in their ads. They were not depicted as window-dressing, rather as students and businesswomen. I hoped this trend signaled the beginnings of a cultural turnaround for women, because fear, or at least intimidation, pervaded even small experiences of women's lives in Kolkata. I'd felt it myself. For example, I was walking to the Internet shop, which is just across the alley from the main door of the Mother House, and a boy, age ten to twelve, raised his hand to grab my breast. In that moment he looked into my face, which—along with my fists—had hardened to a fighting stance. His hand remained suspended, palm open for a couple of seconds as he sized me up, then he snatched his hand away and ran. I'm glad he did, because my reflex would have been less than Christian, and I think he'd have ended up on the ground before I'd even thought about what I was doing. I was totally outraged by his presumption and beyond caring for my fellow man at the moment.

I had to ward off attentions so often that one of my notebooks fell apart. I had been walking with my arms hugging the notebook against my chest in a protective stance, so that the men couldn't reach my breasts. After a couple of blocks, I had sweated all over the notebook and the glue gave way.

At dinner one night, Margaret told me that when the volunteers took the train to see the leper colony, which was located outside of Kolkata, it was so packed that the women could not protect themselves from the men around them.

Margaret said she could hear one female volunteer repeatedly shouting, "Stop it," because some male passengers had their hands all over her. I began to think that the sore throat that kept me from the trip had been a blessing.

Sometimes, the devaluing of women affects the children. It is not uncommon in many countries across the globe to abandon or kill female babies. This and other discriminatory practices have caused a shift in population. In 2001, there were nine hundred twenty seven girls for every thousand boys; that's down from nine hundred forty five in 1991. But the problem caused by devaluing women affected male babies as well. When I was working at the countryside dispensary, I met a woman who asked for powdered milk and vitamin supplements for her baby boy. Sister knew her and asked why she was not breastfeeding the child. The woman replied that her husband did not like the look of her breasts when she was breastfeeding and she was afraid he'd kill her. I'm sure her concerns were valid. In the time I'd been in Kolkata, I'd seen many newspaper stories about women who'd been killed by their husbands. It was a fairly common occurrence, so I didn't doubt her. I was reminded of a billboard I'd seen in Baltimore that gives the numbers of U.S. women who die each year in their own homes. It reads something to the effect of: "Domestic violence. How many will die before we call it murder?" As for the woman at the dispensary—we gave her the powdered milk and pediatric nutritional supplements.

Just as the style of writing in Indian newspapers intrigued me, so did the sound and structure of the spoken language. I had noticed striking similarities between Bengali and Slavic words. Recently, two men who had just been given a meal at *Kalighat* started a fistfight in front of the men's ward. Sister Georgina was shooing them out of the facility, saying what sounded like "*hajda,*" a Serbian word that is pronounced "hiyda." It means "let's go" and "get out of here." I have also heard "*dosto*" in the context that I believed meant "enough." The Slavic root for this word is the same. I looked all over Kolkata for linguistics book about the Sanskrit influence on Slavic languages, but never found one. However, I wrote myself a note to keep it in mind as a future project.

Some English colloquialisms seem to have become universal. For example, just as "okay" has slipped into foreign language, "Oh my God" has inserted itself into Bollywood films. I noticed this on the flight over as well, when we were stopped in Frankfurt. An elderly Vietnamese man kept trying to get off the plane. He did not seem fully oriented. The stewardesses came back and asked his wife to tell him he couldn't disembark in Germany unless he took his passport and all of his carry-on luggage. The wife yelled at him with an irritated voice inflection, and he turned with a dazed look, then ambled slowly back. The woman railed at him in Vietnamese, then suddenly injected, "Oh my God," and lapsed again into Vietnamese.

This memory came back to me when I was having lunch with fellow volunteers Margaret, the eighteen-year-old from Singapore, and Myra Molony, a charming, white-haired British woman, who had retired after owning a restaurant. An outgoing person, she obviously enjoyed people and conversation.

As we were discussing Myra's point that *Kalighat* was not as bad as any of us was expecting and that there were sometimes lines of people waiting to get in for treatment, I was struck by the variations of English spoken at the table. Myra's English was classic British. Margaret had a bit of a Chinese accent and clipped her words, while the Texas in me elongated words, adding extra syllables. The waiters' cadence followed the rhythm of their native Bengali. As our conversations continued, I began to realize that any of us could use common English words and still get quizzical looks from the others.

It's interesting how certain English speakers, and often people who speak English as a second language, enjoy using the present imperfect verb tense that sounds so strange to American ears. Present imperfect is expressed as a process: "I am walking" as opposed to the present tense "I walk." Indians gravitate toward the present imperfect.

Philosophical differences also influence the choice of words. Western philosophy glorifies man. It views him as having power over his environment and being capable of unlocking the secrets of the universe—especially Americans. It therefore follows that American English syntax is oriented toward actions man takes. English sentences follow the pattern of actor, action, and receiver of action.

Indic philosophies see man as caught up in the action and nature as the driving force. Man is acted upon, swept along by a river that moves beyond his control. Sanskrit syntax emphasizes that an action is going on rather than that man is acting. Man is a part of the universe but is neither central nor more powerful or important than other beings.

The books I bought answer some of the questions I'd been pondering since I'd been in Kolkata. Two of the books were Gurcharan Das' *The Elephant Paradigm*[35] and Richard E. Nisbett's *The Geography of Thought: How Asians and Westerners Think Differently...and Why.*[36] Das is an Indian journalist and Nisbett is a psychologist.

Nisbett sees the Asian way of thinking as a series of concentric circles, focusing first on the whole and viewing each part in relation to the whole. The Western system of thought is more of a straight line built from parts that progress to the whole. Westerners have a tendency to examine the parts as separate from the whole. Eastern and Western medical practices reflect this as well. For example, in the U.S., we gravitate towards medical specialties—even nurses do. While it encourages in-depth knowledge in specific fields, it also results in what I call "parts doctors."

For example, several years ago I developed high blood pressure. At the time, I was competing in masters swimming, which included three workouts a week, averaging three thousand five hundred to four thousand meters per workout. The beta-blocker the doctor prescribed for my condition made me become breathless with very small amounts of exercise, such as walking around the house, and I could no longer complete a workout. The medicine also depressed me, causing me to cry when nothing was wrong. When I complained to the doctor, he talked me into taking the pills for another month in hopes that the side effects would subside. After a month I went back and insisted on getting a different medication because the beta-blockers were destroying my life. His response was, "Just stick with it a little longer. They work so well on your blood pressure!" All he could see was that his part of the body had been fixed. He seemed not to realize that I'd lost my ability to enjoy life and it was all due to a medication to which there were many excellent alternatives. Never was I more aware of the need to treat the whole person, as they do in Eastern medicine.

In his *Elephant Paradigm*, Das, an Indian journalist, offers interesting insights on how things work in India. He examines why Southeast Asia has outstripped India in economic growth. He says that Indians put politics before economics, preferring to debate rather than act. He also quotes a businessman who explained why he'd rather do business in Thailand than in India: "I suppose the most important reason is that the Thais want us and they want to learn from us. Indians only want to give us advice." [37] Shades of the lecture I got from the Indian doctor on humility.

In the 1983 preface to his book *Kolkata: The City Revealed*, British author Geoffrey Moorhouse wrote, "One dare not hope for an improvement in Kolkata by more than degrees across long periods of time."[38] Echoing this, Gurcharan Das wrote his opinion as to why economic change comes so slowly to India: "We continue to waste our energies in debating 'the what' when we ought to focus on 'the how'…."[39] This, he says, is the reason that the Government of India has had trouble making plans that can be put into action.

He posits that the leftists who cry constantly for more funding for the poor should put their energies into reforming the distribution programs, so that the poor "actually receive the benefits."[40] He calls "inability to translate thought into action" the real culprit for Indian societal woes. Finally, he points out that between 1965 and 1985, East Asia's economic strategy, and the execution of that strategy, allowed it to grow twice as fast as India.[41]

Long before, Bengali native Rabindranath Tagore wrote of British rule in his *Civilisation and Progress*:

…We have for over a century been dragged by the prosperous West behind its chariot, choked by the dust, deafened by the noise, humbled by our own helplessness, and overwhelmed by the speed. We agreed to acknowledge that this chariot-drive was progress and that progress was civilisation. If we ever ventured to ask, "Progress towards what, and progress for whom?" it was considered to be peculiarly and ridiculously oriental to entertain such doubt about the absoluteness of progress.[42]

Meanwhile, we in the West are dragged behind our own chariots. For example, we see violence as entertainment and power. I'd like to bring those in Hollywood who think violence is such fun here to see what life is really like.

We also tend to be selective in our humanitarian conscience. While in Kolkata, I watched a BBC News Channel documentary about the tenth anniversary of the Rwandan genocide. The speakers emphasized that the British and President Clinton's governments knew what was going on in Rwanda and did nothing, despite the fact that news crews had filmed the action. I understand that it might not have been in the United States' best interest to send troops to Rwanda. I just wish we weren't so sanctimonious about our humanitarian efforts. I wish the government had been honest and said we'd decided to do nothing, instead of saying there was no genocide while a million people died horribly in front of international news cameras. The older I get, the less I believe politicians—any of them.

To a large extent, I think American culture, as magnanimous as it is at times, has lost the art of caring. Mother Teresa believed that we have free will and that doing good deeds is a choice. Giving of self costs us nothing, yet it seems the hardest thing for most of us.

Mother Teresa also desired that those who follow her to work in *Kalighat* live and think like Indians. I have been resistant to this idea, mainly because of my encounters with people who want to maintain status quo in negative ways and condescendingly refer to Westerners as having "new ideas." Personally, I see change as being neither inherently bad nor good— it all depends on the change.

Mother Teresa was a Westerner who made changes with inspired persistence. She did this with great respect for culture and values, but she did not hide her light under a basket. She was a strong leader, like few who have ever walked this earth. What she wanted was for the world to see that God is in each of us and that we should treat each other as we would treat God. This dream has not been realized worldwide, but it was for those she touched, as it continues to be in her Missionaries of Charity and in those for whom they care.

FEELING OUT OF MY DEPTH

I spent the morning at the neurological dispensary that was held in the courtyard of *Shishu Bhavan*. There was no concept of a line at the dispensary, although the sisters were attempting to institute a system of chits for those who were not triaged as emergencies. All the patients had to do was take a chit and they'd be served on a first-come, first-served basis. No one who arrived within working hours would be turned down. However, it was all for naught. I guess the people were used to scrapping for everything, because they just didn't understand that if they took a chit and sat down, we would make sure that they were taken care of, and they wouldn't have to fight their way to the front of the crowd. The men were the worst. They assumed they would be served first just because they were men, but we triaged at clinic to identify and treat the ones in most medical need first. Some of the sisters had to act as guards to fend off those who would not wait or those who were shopping around the stations to get more of something. However, it was difficult for the sisters to be stern—Missionaries of Charity are called to be cheerful, and every one I have ever met has lived up to that.

There was a Muslim woman in a gold lamé cape with a veil. It was the weirdest-looking get-up I've ever seen. She had the physical look of a gypsy, but that was not likely since she was a Muslim. Apparently, she was a regular at the neurological dispensary. She wanted medications that we didn't have and became irritated when I informed her of this. People could get the medications for free at the state hospital but they didn't want to go there. Considering the news articles I'd read about local hospitals and medical practitioners, as well as the counterfeit medications that were floating around that part of the world, I didn't blame them. We had a lot of American samples that had been donated and they knew American-manufactured drugs were reliable.

Some of the women were well dressed but came to the free clinic anyway. One woman brought a boy with a tunneled decubitus ulcer on his buttocks, which is a pressure ulcer that has literally opened a tunnel under the skin. If not cared for properly, the tunnel can expand. It was obviously a long-standing wound because of the white, gristly material around the wound edges. The boy would need surgical debridement to get rid of the gristle and expose tissue that would be capable of closing over. The woman didn't want to take her son to the hospital, however.

Due to the language barrier, I could not determine from the mother how the boy had gotten the wound, but this is the kind of pressure ulcer you see in people who can't move. Being confined to a wheelchair and not being able to move would explain it, but this boy could walk. He was well nourished and well dressed. I knew there was a story behind his condition, but after what I'd seen at *Kalighat*, I didn't want to know what it was.

The children who were brought to dispensary were much older than they looked. Two-year-olds looked like undernourished four—or five-month-olds. These children couldn't walk. Their calves were atrophied, shrunken almost to the bone. Many seemed like they had cerebral palsy—which can occur from a birth trauma—because their legs crossed stiffly and their bodies jerked when they tried to move purposefully. One of these little guys was strikingly emaciated and so listless that he didn't look like he could raise his head. He did not rouse with verbal or gentle physical stimulation. He had tuberculosis.

I gave an intramuscular injection of antibiotics to a boy who did not want to have it. An intramuscular injection in the hip can be dangerous if done wrong. You can't just jab the needle in anywhere, because it is possible to hit the sciatic nerve, which runs down from the lower back along the back of the leg. You have to aim for the upper, outer quadrant of the buttock. I'm proficient in finding the right spot in an adult, but it was intimidating to try to adjust my aim on this squirming child.

Antibiotic shots are big, and I wanted to inject quickly so that I wouldn't damage the nerve if he moved. But penicillin takes a while, because the serum is viscous. His mother was holding him still, but in the middle of the injection, he tensed his muscles. When he clamped down, the syringe disengaged from the needle and penicillin blew back onto my face and shirt. I grabbed the needle out of his little cheek before he damaged himself by wiggling it around, and I figured he'd had enough for one day.

One woman had symptoms of appendicitis, but she vehemently refused to go to the hospital. I spent a lot of time with an interpreter trying to explain that she was endangering her life by delaying treatment. I told her I would give her three acetaminophen tablets but that they would only supply a little relief to tide her over while she waited for treatment at the hospital. Even after all that, I did not feel reassured that she would go. She was obviously afraid.

The Hindustan Times reported a story that helps explain the woman's attitude. It seems that a woman had to give birth outside a hospital because the on-call doctor was sleeping and refused to admit her. After giving birth, she had to lie outside on the ground for another five hours before she could be transported to another hospital. Her husband had taken the twenty-five-year old woman to the Habra Hospital at three-thirty in the morning. He had to bribe a guard to even get into the emergency department, and once there, he begged for half an hour to get someone to awaken the on-call doctor, Tapash Sarkar.

When Dr. Sarkar finally came to the emergency department, he took a cursory look at the laboring woman and decided not to treat her. Instead, he wrote a note saying she was to be transferred to Barasat hospital and then went back to sleep. Of course, there was no ambulance or other form of transport, so her husband tried to drag her back out into the yard in front of the hospital. She was writhing in pain and sobbing loudly. Eventually, relatives of other patients helped him lay his wife out on the grounds. They advised him to let her deliver there because further movement at this point might kill her.

Fortunately, a midwife from the woman's village arrived at the hospital just before the baby was born. Nevertheless, the woman delivered amidst a crowd of onlookers—a humiliating experience for a modest Indian woman—then she had to lie on the ground outside the hospital without medical care for the rest of the night. At dawn, a mob of villagers who had heard about what had happened the night before ransacked the hospital, dragged Dr. Tapash Sarkar outside, and beat him until the police came to his rescue.[43]

The arrogance of doctors can be a problem in the United States too. Before I left for Kolkata, I read a book that criticized Mother Teresa and her facilities. It featured an American doctor who did not approve of the care the sisters gave. He said they could better serve the poor by devoting their energies to healthcare activism and said they should just take people to hospitals and demand their right to treatment rather than providing care that is different from hospital standards.

First of all, the sisters did send patients to the hospital—when broken bones were suspected, for example—but those patients didn't necessarily come back in better shape. I believe that the newspaper articles I read throughout my month in Kolkata speak to the issue of why people don't fight to get into hospitals that don't want them. Among the stories were scandals about unlicensed doctors killing people, on-call doctors not willing to get out of bed to treat emergencies, medical schools accepting bribes for admissions, appalling hospital conditions, and negligent care. Such occurrences make it clear why the sisters continue to provide an alternative to the "free" medical care system provided by the government.

Still, one big lesson I'd learned in Kolkata was that different does not equate to better or worse. The trip reinforced that hospital services are not equal and not all medical personnel are competent or care about their patients—and I include the U.S. in that statement. When I fell ill in Kolkata, even though I had plenty of insurance, I took care of myself. I wouldn't even go to get a throat culture, chest x-ray, or tuberculosis skin test, which could have been a catastrophic miscalculation. The truth is that I did not trust the system enough to see a doctor there.

This criticism that the sisters should spend their time taking patients to the hospital instead of caring for them at home came back to me when I was back in Baltimore at Christmas. I had been packing food for needy families at the Missionaries of Charity hospice, and we were running low on canned milk. We were down to a bunch of bent cans. Without them, we didn't have enough to give everyone a bag. I shrugged my shoulders and said, "What the heck? Some is better than none," then started tossing bent cans into bags.

A young man I was working with stopped me. He didn't criticize; he just asked, "Would you give that milk to your baby?"

All I had considered was that we needed more milk, not whether what I was about to provide to the poor was good enough. Based upon his question, it was not.

My conclusion about whether the sisters should spend their time advocating that hospitals take destitute patients because any hospital is better than no hospital is: if it's not good enough for me or my family, it's not good enough for my patients. Given the choice, I'd choose *Kalighat* over hospitals that didn't want me.

Back at *Kalighat* the next morning, I continued to struggle over the case of Kshama, the psychotic woman with the infected arm that was shedding skin in parchment-like sheets from mid-forearm to fingertips. Today, her hand was swollen to at least twice normal size, and the skin that was clinging to the fingers had split open. Profuse pus oozed through the breaks in the skin. I'd originally thought it might be a staph infection, because of the scalded appearance and the fact that the skin was peeling off as if removing a glove. But having researched what Liz had said about mycobacteria, I was beginning to think it was cutaneous TB, which can proceed from respiratory TB, which is what we see in the West. In fact, I'd never seen cutaneous TB in my clinical practice, only in pictures on the Internet.

Kshama's infection had not responded to penicillin or gentamycin, a strong antibiotic that works against a broad spectrum of bacterial infections. Heaven knows the woman was emaciated enough to have advanced tuberculosis or AIDS or both. I'd spent two hours on the Internet trying to find pictures that might give me a clue as to the cause, but I couldn't find anything that looked prurient enough. How I missed Liz and the doctors from Oregon. I'd only met them that one day, but I trusted them and wished for their counsel.

I decided to send an email query to an international wound-care network to canvass other nurses for help. A nurse from Brazil wrote back with suggestions. Among the points she made was: "For most wound specialists that have not practiced in regions away from the best resources and supplies offered by most wound clinics, this can really raise hairs!" I was reassured by this statement, because I knew she wasn't going to give me a high-tech solution.

She told me about a wound she'd seen that started from a spider bite. The family had picked at in an attempt to release the pus that had formed at the site of the bite wound. All they did was introduce more infective organisms, and the secondary infection caused the arm to swell so badly that it choked off the blood and thereby the oxygen supply to the skin. Ulcers formed, and the arm ended up looking like Kshama's. In the end, what had cured the Brazilian patient were standard woundcare procedures and finding the right antibiotic.

I guess I kept thinking of TB because there was so much of it in Kolkata. I knew I would need to get a couple of TB tests myself when I got home. I wasn't coughing, but most of my patients had tuberculosis, and it takes up to ninety days for symptoms to develop. I had been comforting myself with the hope that I might be somewhat genetically resistant to tuberculosis, because my father and aunt both survived it when they were young and, on several occasions, I'd been exposed to AIDS-related TB quite closely and had still tested negative.

The first man I ever shaved was an AIDS patient in a hospice where I volunteered. He had been tested for tuberculosis because of a persistent cough, but the lab results had come back negative.

I took hot water into his room, soaked some washcloths in it, and then applied them to his face. After that, I soaped him up and began shaving. I moved slowly, because I was afraid of cutting him, and he had a deep cough that gripped his body in deep spasms and increased the chances that I would draw blood. I was so proud of myself when we finished what turned out to be a bloodless procedure, but when I walked out of his room, a nurse approached me, looking pale and agitated. The lab had called in a panic to say that they'd called in the wrong results the day before. The patient did have TB and would have to be isolated. That was over a decade ago and only the first of several such mishaps.

It happened again when I was a nursing student in my public health rotation. I was caring for an AIDS patient in Baltimore, whose main problem was his legs. He had an advanced stage of venous insufficiency, and the skin on his lower legs was like tree bark. I had to inspect the legs and help him put on compression stockings, which is not a simple task because they fit tightly to keep the blood from pooling in the lower leg and forming clots. To do this, the patient sat on a chair and I kneeled on the roach-infested floor of his subsidized apartment and struggled for quite some time to pull those things onto his legs. Over the period of two weeks, he developed a cough, which progressed to night sweats and coughing up blood. I sent him to the free clinic to be evaluated, and sure enough, it was TB he'd been coughing in my face while I helped with those stockings.

Such events explain why so many healthcare workers test positive for TB exposure. So far, I'd been lucky.

Other than being baffled by Kshama's condition, the day went pretty well. In fact, I'd had a little chuckle, mostly at my own expense, for being such a practical-minded Western nurse. I had awakened that morning with a vaginal yeast infection. I always get them when I take antibiotics. This is a common phenomenon in women, because there are good bacteria that live in the female reproductive tract and keep the chemicals balanced, but antibiotics kill the good bacteria with the bad. Once the good bacteria die, *candidiasis*, also known as a yeast infection, can develop.

One of the novices had been put on antibiotics for sore throat. Spurred on by my own experience, I tried to explain to her about using vaginal suppositories for *candidiasis*, but she didn't seem to be catching the concept. I began to realize that no one had ever discussed the workings of the female anatomy with her. As a nurse, I felt morally bound to remedy this situation immediately. I tried to get one of the older sisters to come back with me to translate, but she got the giggles and told me to forget it, because the novice would not use a vaginal suppository under any circumstances. I don't know why it didn't occur to me that nuns would object to what I see as purely medical—having absolutely nothing to do with sex—but it didn't. At least I ensured that she wouldn't take the vaginal suppository as an oral dose.

MONUMENTS TO LIFE

I finally got a chance to visit the historic cemetery I'd passed on my travels to Park Street. The South Circular Street Cemetery is the only surviving eighteenth-century British cemetery. Contrary to how it appeared from the street, it was largely ruined and overgrown.

It was filled with ornate monuments, but the tributes that had been carved upon them were mostly unreadable, because the text had been pelted away by decades—for some, more than a century—of Kolkata sands and acrid pollution. These were proud symbols of forgotten persons and deeds. Some epitaphs said they were well loved. Were they? Some bore lofty titles, yet the significance of those titles was long forgotten. Stones were tipped over and cracked, and the jungle was reclaiming the space. Of the stones that could be read, I was struck by the numbers of infants and toddlers: one day, one month, one year.

It was a contemplative afternoon, and I walked up and down the rows in the thirty-five degree Celsius heat, which is ninety-five degrees Fahrenheit. Rain clouds cast a gray haze across the sky, and the humidity made the air feel like I could almost push it with my hands. Green vines with yellow flowers curled around the stones and invaded the walkways, while crows dive-bombed passersby. As I walked between two crypts, a mango dropped from a tree and rapped me on the back of the head. Dogs slept on the raised-platform mausoleums.

What I saw that day only hinted at the grandeur that once was the

British Empire. But those who were so important in those times had become a curiosity.

There was justice in this slow overtaking by the silent green blanket of jungle that crept across the field and all that was in it. From the streets, the never-abating blast of horns was a glaring reminder that what I saw in this cemetery was a time gone by. Still, I hated to see this shattered and eroded history, if for no other than esthetic reasons.

I was jolted from my thoughts by a male voice that demanded, "You give me money." I turned to see a well-nourished teen in reasonably respectable dress. "Hello," he insisted. "No father. You give me money."

"Sorry," I said and walked away. He was too well fed to be in need of a handout. I took Mother's advice and did not contribute to this boy's place in the cycle of poverty and crime.

The situation reminded me of a friend who graduated from Yale Law School and became an Assistant United States Attorney. His career dream was to gain enough prosecutive experience to fully understand the criminal justice system and then become a good public defender. He was willing to sacrifice a lucrative position to do this.

After I left the FBI in 1990, he left the United States Attorney's Office and followed this dream. I saw him a year or so later and asked what he thought of his move. He shook his head and grappled for the right words, and then looked me in the eye. "I'm sick of being lied to by drug dealers and con artists," was his disheartened response. In this cemetery, his words rang true to me. It was not that I'd lost my sympathy or become complacent to the plight of the poor; rather, I recognized the difference between helping and enabling.

The current of life ebbs and flows in Kolkata: the traffic, the crowds—though even at low tide, neither fully disappears, just as Indian life did not vanish under colonial oppression. The graveyard signified to me that who we are—or who we think we are—does not endure in this world. We may leave children and grandchildren when we go, along with people whom we touched, but not much more. Our monuments and achievements will be forgotten.

What will I leave the world when I depart this life? I guess we've all pondered that question. For me, there on the shores of the Ganges, the answer was clear: two children, who will have children, who will have children.

I thought about the nuns at Mother Teresa's house. Generations from now, they may not be remembered as individuals, but I have no doubt that the order and their work will be. They, unlike most of us, would prefer it that way, and while they would never ask that their story be recorded, I would like to do so. I was once told that the best story is one of ordinary people doing extraordinary things. This describes the Missionaries of Charity: they are ordinary men and women, but their work is nothing short of extraordinary.

When Mother Teresa told her own mother she wanted to give her life to God, her mother said, "My daughter, if you begin something, begin it wholeheartedly. Otherwise, don't begin it at all..." This became her philosophy and her demand of those who chose to follow her path.

It was important to Mother Teresa that she lived as the poor and counted on God alone for her income. The Missionaries of Charity do not allow professional fund-raising or accept money from the Catholic Church. They live on what they can bring in themselves, and while they get a lot of donations, they don't live sumptuously or finance grand buildings. They use the money to open more homes that provide basic necessities to those in need.

Mother Teresa clearly stated her goals when she accepted the Nobel Prize for Peace: "And with this prize that I have received as a prize of peace, I am going to try to make the home for many people that have no home." Homes where they could heal the poor were what the Missionaries of Charity set out to provide, and that is what they continue to do.

A statue of Mother stands outside her tomb in the walled courtyard where the volunteers gather for breakfast. Her feet are bare, bunioned, and wrinkled. The texture of her hands and face is also wrinkled. I doubt that she is five feet tall—though her shoulders are a little stooped, which may make her seem shorter. A simple wooden rosary hangs from her hands, which are brought together in prayer or in the *namaskar*, the Hindu sign of greeting and respect.

In photographs, her skin is weathered brown, wrinkled, and frail as parchment. But on her face is the smile that illuminates those around her even now. When Mother Teresa's spirit prevails, there is joy in service.

In the room where we had mass was a life-sized statue of the tiny Mother Teresa, seated on the ground, her legs tucked around to one side, and her head bowed in prayer. It is so lifelike that I didn't realize it wasn't a person until I arrived early one evening and noticed she didn't move. Only then did I recognize that the facial color favored mannequin more than woman.

I often sat at the foot of Mother's tomb when I needed to think. It reminded me of sitting near the much larger-than-life-sized statue of Jesus in The Johns Hopkins Hospital Administrative Building before nursing shifts. It is a particularly beautiful statue that is carved from marble but has enormous feet that always drew my attention. Christ reaches out to passers-by as if to enfold them in his arms, and he always gave me the sense of peace that I needed to go back for one more shift in the ICU. One of my nursing school professors told me that she, too, went there to pray before each ICU shift. Medical practice in the United States changes quickly in scientific knowledge, pharmaceuticals, as well as technologies that show up on the nursing floor. Usually, nurses get "trained" on new technologies with a demonstration and maybe a little practice before you have to use it on patients. Due to this, my professor, a highly experienced and competent nurse, went to the statue before shifts and prayed that she would not make a mistake that would kill anyone. This became my fervent prayer as well.

A point of interest about the statue is that Hopkins was established in a time when only religious hospitals were considered reliable. The Johns Hopkins Hospital was non-sectarian and had trouble drawing customers, so the statue was placed in the main building to make people think it was a religious hospital.

Mother's tomb is not grand like the edifices of Johns Hopkins medicine; it is a simple rectangular box of white marble that is so plain I thought it was made of concrete until someone told me otherwise. It occupies a few square feet on one side of a room that is unfurnished, save for the wooden benches that line the walls. The walls themselves are beige, and the gray concrete floor is riddled with fissures. The tomb is just high enough to pray next to on your knees, and in this room, silence is observed, except for the occasional mass.

Her headstone reads: "Love one another as I have loved you. (St. John 15: 12)." It's a simple idea, but not so simple to carry out. The top of the tomb was always decorated in the orange-gold marigolds that were sold on the street, strung into garlands. The sisters pulled the petals from the blooms and piled them into words or simple pictures. One day, they formed the words "A clean heart can see God." Another day, the flowers read "Jesus—Homeless to be taken in," and there was a house fashioned from flowers above the words.

One evening, I attended a small mass at Mother's tomb that was led by an Australian priest. The sisters sat on the floor with their legs curved to the side in the posture Mother preferred. The post-Easter mass liturgy was much more like the standard Lutheran mass, and I was able to say most of it from memory.

Introducing the sermon, the priest told a joke that I couldn't hear. No one laughed. After a painful pause, he said, "That was a joke." Still no one laughed, so he cleared his throat and moved on. I felt sorry for him. For most of the people in the room, English was a second language. Getting jokes in a foreign language is sometimes difficult.

As the sisters' voices united in song, I so wanted to follow their example—not to be a nun, but to be of service to others and not care so much about my own needs. I knew that I would backslide, but it buoyed me up to try to follow their example. They seemed so happy all the time, giggling like schoolgirls when they talked together. How wonderful that Mother realized that cheerfulness makes people want to be a part of the work and that it's okay to enjoy being a nun.

That evening, Mother's tomb was decorated in gold and white flowers. The gold flowers formed the word "Alleluia," and there was a candle in the center. I prayed a long time, kneeling next to the tomb and touching the rosary Jane gave me to it, so I would be able to remember all this when I looked at the rosary. While I don't venerate saints, I see the grace in the example Mother set. It helps me to think on these things while I pray to God to ask him to guide my actions, and it makes me less judgmental. Not being judgmental is a hard one for me, but it is a vital skill in nursing.

Kolkata demonstrated how rewarding it can be to explore complexities and not base judgments upon quick looks. It is a city of many layers, with much of life set back from the street, behind walls and gates and secluded internal passageways. There was a symbiosis of odd things that just seemed to fit in that city. Trees grew out of crumbling stucco on the sides of buildings that abutted the Mother House. Eroded areas in the stucco revealed beautiful brickwork with arches, three bricks across, over the window ledges.

The high walls and ventilation in the Missionaries of Charity courtyard offered refuge from the heat. Breezes accelerated when they slid down the courtyard walls. While I would have expected the walls to keep the wind out, instead it was an effective configuration for comfort.

The sisters don't sleep with fans, because Mother didn't use them. They turned the fans in the Mother House on when visitors came, then turned them off when the visitors were gone. Because the order is growing, the Missionaries of Charity were adding to their living space at the Mother House. The windows were blocked with decorative iron grillwork. It was obvious that there would be no air-conditioning in the new wing either.

As Mother taught them, the sisters blend with the culture around them, adhering to the simplest ways. At the Mother House, as at the homes where patients were treated, they scrubbed the floors and concrete court-yard on their hands and knees every day—more often, if need be. They first swept it with hand brooms that resembled bundles of straw with one end folded over and wrapped to work as a handle. To use these brooms, the sisters had to bend in half or crouch. This is not an easy task, but no one complained, because they believe as Mother Teresa did: "I do nothing. He does it all. I am a little pencil in God's Hand. He does the thinking. He does the movement. I have only to be the pencil..."

Working with the sisters reminded me that there are many wonderful people on this earth who let you see God through their actions. To me, this is true evangelism. I admire them for this, although admiration is not what they seek. Their example has redirected my thoughts from the mundane problems of my comfortable life to those of the humanity that is so easy to overlook if you don't specifically seek it. For this I will be eternally grateful.

In Kolkata, I decided to find a way to volunteer in world humanitarian programs as often as possible. I still work fulltime, so it will take some planning. My dream is to work for a month in Cambodia. I could work with the Missionaries of Charity in their AIDS hospice in the morning and, hopefully, an AIDS education program for sex workers in the afternoon or evening. Living in India has sensitized me to the number of women and girls who are sold into the sex trade worldwide, to the cruelty and lack of rights that women endure every day in the far reaches of the world.

When asked what she would do if poverty were eliminated from the earth, Mother responded she'd be out of a job. Wouldn't that be wonderful?

BEGINNING OF THE END

Morning mass was inspiring, partly because I went to Mother's tomb to pray before the service started and was filled with peaceful thoughts. The marigold petals on the tomb said, "Something beautiful for God," an apt description of the work done here.

I have to admit that I was feeling like I'd let the *Kalighat* patients down while I was having a good time in the dispensaries. I realized that they, like all hospice patients, were in precarious health and that their conditions could change from hour to hour without warning. Nothing drives that point home more than coming back to this intense nursing floor from a couple of days' respite.

When I returned to the women's ward, Anuradha's abdomen looked like she was about to deliver a baby. Someone had removed her urinary catheter, and the tip of her bladder was swollen above the umbilicus. She was writhing in pain. When she saw me, she held out her arms and frantically called to me. Though paralyzed from the waist down, she struggled to roll off the cot, as if she were trying to crawl to me. I ran to her and touched her belly to let her know I understood what was going on. When I cathed her, I took off more than two liters immediately. I emptied another one and a half liters during the four-hour shift. During the two days I was away at dispensary, they were treating her for gas, because her stomach was distended. I felt selfish for not having been there to intercede for her.

A fever was spreading through the women's ward. The affected patients' temperatures ranged from around one hundred one to one hundred two degrees. Only three of the patients' beds were in close proximity.

Anuradha had a lot of white sediment in her urine, which meant she probably had a urinary tract infection. This could account for her elevation in temperature, but she also had swollen glands just beneath the jaw between her chin and ears. Swollen glands indicate infection, and since lymph glands are placed throughout the body and can generally be thought of as draining an infected area that is above them, it was likely that the location of infection was ears, nose, or throat. This, too, could account for her fever. I started a regimen of azithromycin, the antibiotic that had worked so wonderfully for me when my sore throat put me out of commission for a couple of days.

A new patient on a nearby cot was in respiratory distress and was vomiting. Still another had fever and no additional obvious symptoms, but she was also a stroke victim and could not speak, so I couldn't evaluate her well.

Yet another had blisters scattered sporadically on her face, arms, back, and trunk. I heard that Liz, the doctor from America, had come back for a day while I was at dispensary. She'd had a chance to look at the blisters and didn't think it was varicella. Unfortunately, the person who was telling me about Liz's opinion was not medically trained and didn't speak much English, so she was not able to recall what Liz did think it was. The blisters did seem too few to be varicella (chicken pox), and they didn't look like burns or anything else I had seen. I was at a loss as to what to do about them, and I left for lunch knowing I had some Internet research ahead of me. By then I was emailing nurses at Johns Hopkins and the National Institutes of Health whenever I felt stumped—or sometimes when I just needed reassurance.

While at lunch, Myra—the retired restaurateur from London—told Phillis and me the most astonishing story. That morning, Myra and a French volunteer named Maria had walked to *Prem Dan*, the home that serves long-term patients who are not severe enough for Kalighat. As they crossed, they saw a passenger train coming from one side. Suddenly, an elderly Indian woman started yelling for them to get down. That's when they noticed a train approaching from the opposite direction and realized that they were trapped in the narrow space between two sets of tracks.

The Indian woman threw her arms around Myra and dragged her to the ground so that the force of the passing trains would not suck her onto the tracks. As she lay on the ground, locomotives thundering around her, Myra heard Maria call. She looked up and Maria snapped her picture.

As Myra stared in disbelief, realizing how precarious their situation was and frightened nearly out of her wits, Maria shouted, "I'm not sure the picture's going to come out!" Apparently, that was all she was worried about.

Myra was still shaken as she bared her soul to Phillis and me, but instead of comforting her, we both burst into laughter. In fact, we laughed so hard we could not catch our breath. It was one of those laughs borne of exhaustion, heat, and an outrageously bizarre experience. By coincidence I later read in *The Hindustan Times* that an average of one hundred forty one people per year are killed at Kolkata railway crossings.

My return to *Kalighat* after lunch was tinged with sadness. Bina, the poor respiratory patient who the four doctors said was faking it, and who had been in almost continual respiratory distress since the Bengali New Year, died. As it turned out, she had tuberculosis and asthma. As a hospice nurse and volunteer, I'd seen many deaths, but this one left me particularly unsettled. I felt like I should have done more, but I didn't know what.

Anjali, the little one who had been beaten and raped, eloped from the facility, and another young girl had been discharged. The patient population was ever changing.

In their place, I discovered a respiratory patient who was also vomiting. She crouched on the bed on her elbows and knees, her arms forming the characteristic respiratory tripod that eases the weight off the lungs to allow them to expand easier. She was in bad shape. The sound of the fluid bubbling in her lungs was too loud for me to even hear her heart beat. Her heart rate, which I knew from her pulse, was firing at high speed like a piston in a racing car. Because of this, she was frantically gulping oxygen from the ancient canister that Bina no longer needed. She'd had her inhaler and an extra shot of theophylline, so I gave her prochlorperazine, an antiemetic to ease the nausea, and—I hoped—help calm her down. Prochlorperazine tends to induce sleep, and fortunately, it worked for her. After about twenty minutes, her rate of breathing slowed somewhat, probably because she stopped vomiting and was less panicked.

I'd heard that she had longstanding TB and did not take her medications when she was on her own. While I had no idea how to cure her, hospice had taught me to focus on comfort measures when there is no cure. So at least I could halt the nausea and help her get some sleep.

Meanwhile, there was a wonderful victory: Jaya, the lady with elephantiasis, went home. Apparently she owned property but had been out one day and, overcome by illness, had fallen in the street. She was brought to the Missionaries of Charity. It had taken a while to find her family, but now they had come to take her home.

When she left, Jaya was wearing a pastel yellow, gauzy-looking sari with flowers embroidered along the border. She was gingerly making her way on elephantine legs, but with great dignity. There was something regal in her bearing. Head held high, she said her goodbyes as she progressed down the aisle of friends with whom she'd spent the last month.

This story could have ended very differently, with Jaya stranded on the streets of Kolkata, succumbing to infection or crime. But the sisters saved her and gave her back her dignity along with her life. Jaya was living proof that cleanliness, good nutrition, and a safe and respectful environment go a long way in promoting healing.

Since the antipsychotic haloperidol dose was beginning to take affect, the change in Kshama—the lady with the infected arm that was shedding its skin—has been profound. She had gone from darkly paranoid, constantly threatening, her eyeballs distended from the sockets, to laughing and hugging, infected arm and all. Her humor was genuine. Although an ocean of language separated us, I could see that her laughter was responsive and appropriate. Lately, when we nurses hurried by, Kshama pointed and giggled. I'm sure the looks on our faces as we swam against the torrent of blind diagnoses and polyglot pharmacy were comedic to watch day-in and day-out. And she had a ringside seat. What did she really think? I wondered.

The day also brought another humbling experience. I noticed that a woman was sweating profusely, a condition known as diaphoresis. In general, diaphoresis is an ominous sign, so I knew I had to attend to her as an emergency.

When I touched her, her skin was cool and clammy, and she was difficult to arouse. Her breathing was fine, and my first thought was that the diaphoresis meant something serious was going wrong with her heart.

She was a slip of a woman, about forty years old, and had been fully conscious the last time I'd passed her cot. I took her pulse, which was sixty and regular. She was not fibrillating, but I needed much more information to figure out why she was diaphoretic.

I had to find someone to translate for me so that I could ask questions. Just then, Australian nurse Susan walked by and asked what was happening. The look on her face darkened to alarm and she told me that the patient was a diabetic. Susan went off to find a glucometer to measure the woman's blood glucose levels, another instrument I hadn't seen since I'd been there. She took the blood sugar and announced, "She's low. Stay with her while I get some sugar."

By the time Susan came back, the woman was delirious, and I didn't need to understand her words to realize it. Granulated sugar was nowhere to be found, so Susan dissolved some sweet biscuits in milk and returned with the glop. The patient would have none of it.

One of the novices who spoke Bengali came over and tried to talk the patient into eating some of the sugary mix, but the woman was beyond reason. We had to get the sugar into her or she could die, and she was too healthy for us to allow that to happen.

Ketoacidosis is a condition that can progress to a diabetic coma because the body can no longer take up insulin and thus can no longer process glucose. Lacking glucose for fuel, the body metabolizes fat and produces ketones. Ketones are acids that can build up in the blood when there isn't enough insulin. Essentially, too many ketones poison the body by making the blood more acidic than the body's tissues. This condition can result in death. Signs include behavior that is so irrational that is can be mistaken for drunkenness or a drug high, and this woman was out of control. We had to get some sugar into her to provide a rush of glucose and slow her steady march towards diabetic coma and death.

When in control of her faculties, she knew we meant her no harm, but now she batted at Susan's hands and rolled her head back and forth so Susan could not put the food in her mouth. Since she was refusing to cooperate, the only recourse was to force feed her while she still remained conscious enough to swallow. In this situation, I agreed.

Several more nurses came over, then someone remembered that an American doctor had come in for the morning and was feeding a patient on the men's side. I ran over and got him. By then, the woman was seizing and a crowd of volunteers had gathered. Someone was injecting phenytoin intravenously to get the seizure under control, and a bubble was rising from the crook of the patient's elbow. The vein had burst. Still, after a couple of minutes, the seizure calmed and the woman slept. The next time I saw her, she was sitting up and chatting with friends.

Everything cycled at *Kalighat*—the volunteers, the patients, the medications that were available. But some constants remained: the inexplicable understanding of non-medically trained volunteers from all over the world who proved every day that human touch heals. This is something we know at hospice too. We also know that when the hands of this world can't bring about healing, unseen hands step in.

Hospice patients showed me time and time again that those who precede us in death are always near, and so it will be with my friends from *Kalighat*. The patients, the volunteers, and of course, the Missionaries of Charity will be with me in my heart.

I've said I'm a Doubting Thomas (the Apostle who saw Christ after his resurrection but refused to believe it until he stuck his hands in Christ's wounds), but there's nothing like working with dying patients to help you believe in what you can't see. Before they die, people tend to come to a resolution that gives peace so profound that it must be the Biblical peace that passes understanding.

It is important to listen to the words of the dying and seriously ill, because they often tell you what they see of the place they are going, and they also give hints of when they will die. This was another reason the language barrier in India was so hard for me. I was accustomed to talking with patients about what happens when death approaches, and I felt sorry I was not able to do that with the patients at *Kalighat*. I wondered how the perspective I would have gotten from them would have differed from those I'd met in the past.

I usually prepared patients and families by telling them what would happen physiologically when death approached and how it would look to them. For some it is comforting to know that death from sustained illness is a process of slowing down. At first the changes are subtle. People usually sleep more as the body wears down. They eat less as the body ceases to process food well, and the bowels slow, as do the kidneys. Blood pressure falls, and for a time the heart rate quickens, but eventually, the heart rate calms too.

Along with the cardiac changes, a breathing pattern ensues wherein the patient appears to hold his breath for a while, then takes several rapid breaths to recover. This is called Cheyne-Stokes breathing. Unnecessary blood vessels close down as the body shunts blood to the vital organs. This, combined with decreased breathing rate, causes the skin—especially the extremities—to turn blue. As the Cheyne-Stokes breathing progresses, the periods of apnea—when the person does not breathe—become longer and the recovery breaths fewer and more shallow, until it all slows to a stop.

There are those few who die panting, but I've only seen two or three in fourteen years of observing hospice patients. Everyone else passed gently from this life into the next.

Some in the medical profession say the visions of the dying are hallucinations. I don't believe that—their words are too specific, too similar from one patient to the other. Yet each vision is tailored to the patient's life. Also, I'm certain it is not the drug or the disease causing the visions, because the response is universal across diseases, and it occurs without drugs.

Someone from the other side comes for them—usually someone they love, but sometimes it is a stranger. This is the beginning of peace and the dying process. At hospice, it was part of shift-change report to say whether anyone were having "heavenly conversations." You'd walk into a room and try to talk to a patient, but he would speak over your shoulder—and not necessarily out loud. This was what we called a heavenly conversation. Sometimes patients asked in exasperation, "Don't you see him?"

Heavenly conversations were rarely understandable, but they marked a stage in the dying process. Women who have lost children often see babies. There was even a young boy described by a number of patients in one hospice. The patients said he was looking in their windows and calling to them. They described the same physical attributes, but over the years, his age never changed. The nurses had searched to find whether a boy fitting that description either lived nearby or had died on the land where the hospice was built, but his identity remained a mystery.

The mind has a lot to do with the date when we die from illness. People set specific goals they want to achieve before they die—to live until Christmas, a birthday, a graduation. It is so common that asking whether special dates are approaching has become part of the hospice admitting process, and there is always a sudden increase of deaths after major holidays.

A cancer patient in one of the hospices where I worked, whose son was graduating from college, kept saying that he just had to live to see his son graduated. Hospice does its best to grant wishes, so an ambulance had been arranged to take him to the graduation ceremony. The day arrived, but he took a turn for the worse and was unable to go. The family wanted to remember everything in scrupulous detail, so they videotaped the ceremony, and the video recorded the time. The man died only a few minutes after his son walked across the stage to accept his diploma.

I also took care of a young woman who had joked with her brother for months leading up to her death that she was going to die "when her number was up." The two were fanatical lottery players, and "her number" became her brother's birth date.

The night before his birthday, she slipped into a coma. When I said goodbye to her at the end of my shift, she was Cheyne-Stoking—the breathing pattern that occurs near death—and her fingernails were navy blue, which meant her body had closed down the small blood vessels in the extremities to shunt blood to the vital organs. Never in my wildest dreams did I expect to find her alive when I walked in the next morning, but there she was. Her brother arrived at about eight o'clock, and the woman died within the hour.

Our attitudes and beliefs profoundly affect how we die. Mother Teresa wanted everyone to live—and die—with dignity. As simple a thought as that is, everything about Western medicine goes against it. When you become a patient in a hospital, they take your clothes. You are given medications according to the hospital's schedule, not necessarily when you want them. If you need assistance to the bathroom, you must wait until someone has taken care of the higher priorities and has time to help you. They may even put you in adult diapers and ask you to go in them instead of getting up.

I remember a hospice patient who was in her seventies. She was in the advanced stages of cancer and could not get around. To make matters worse, she had become incontinent of bowel, as most do at the end of life. One day, I was changing her after she'd had a bout of diarrhea and she began to cry. I asked her what was wrong and she said, "I'm seventy-three and I'm having my diapers changed." I assured her that it was no trouble for me and that the incontinence was due to her disease, not her toileting habits, but she continued to cry. She felt completely demoralized. After I finished, I sat with her until she went to sleep. Exhausted and ravaged by disease as she was, it did not take long.

Disease and dying take so much from us as humans, and we in the highly advanced world of Western medicine need to slow down and examine our own humanity. It takes little enough to reinforce a patient's self-respect, so why is it not a top priority? Sometimes it seems we in the healthcare business think that giving a patient the benefit of our superior skills is good enough for them and they should be grateful for the few moments we bestow upon them as we run from task to task.

Among other things, my time with the Missionaries of Charity has taught me that true miracles occur when we let others see that we care. In the presence of love, the spirit can find the power to heal the body without the latest medical advances.

BETWEEN TWO WORLDS

I decided to attend a Protestant service this evening at the Circular Road Baptist Church. It was founded in 1821 and is located across the street from my hotel. I arrived early, only to find the gates still locked.

It was dusk, and the clouds were gray-tinged, with robin's-egg-blue sky peeking through. A dozen small birds played in the air, riding the pressure pockets as the ubiquitous crows dive-bombed targets of opportunity on the streets. I watched the birds, the sky, and the beehive of traffic, taking in the sounds and textures. Things looked different in the evenings—a little cleaner, a little cooler. I wanted to remember the details and translate these feelings into words.

After fifteen minutes, the church gates opened, and I entered the sanctuary. My immediate impression, once I was seated inside, was that it reminded me of Hawaii. The vegetation was thick and lush through the windows, and wall-sized double doors stood open every few pews, revealing gold-stuccoed outbuildings with Williamsburg-blue trim. Birds flew freely from the gardens and into the sanctuary.

I was so used to taking my shoes off at the Missionaries of Charity that I felt odd wearing them into the church—so much so that even when I noticed the pastor did not remove his shoes, I didn't feel comfortable entering. Instead, I walked back to the gate to double-check whether the congregation was allowed to wear shoes. Finally, reassured by the gate guards, I went in.

Once inside, I found that the décor was mahogany, with wicker chairs, a black baby grand, an organ, and an ornately carved mahogany lectern. My eyes fell on a collection plate, which is not something you'd see at the Missionaries of Charity. On the wall hung marble scrolls memorializing pastors since the 1800s. The founder of this church was born in the 1700s in Birmingham, England. He arrived in Kolkata in 1814. A Swiss pastor was born in 1811. He arrived in Kolkata in 1839 and died in 1880.

The musty-smelling hymnal had been ravaged, as if worms had crawled in and eaten trails through it. Hymns were posted. First up was "Rock of Ages," a personal favorite of mine, followed by "Jesus Calls Us o'er the Tumult." I love these old hymns and am a bit sad that they've faded from American church services in favor of modern tunes.

As the service started, the Muslim call to prayer sounded. Birds flew through the sanctuary, and the sun had fully set by six-twenty. I was caught between worlds. There was no place to kneel, but the songs were familiar. However, when we started to sing, the congregation's voices competed with each other. I found myself wincing. The sermon was nice and I left the church humming "Draw me nearer, nearer precious Lord," but thirsting for something I did not find there.

Outside, I greeted two pastors: the Baptist and a Lutheran. They told me the times when their services were held and invited me to attend, but I knew I would not. The worship that fulfilled me was service to the patients. This was tangible Christianity and I, like Doubting Thomas, had a need to feel Christ's wounds to believe.

For all I didn't understand about the Catholic Church as a Protestant, the emphasis on service to those in need is a quality I embraced. There was a sign posted in Mother's tomb reminding us:

> Ye are the light of the world. A city that is set on a hill cannot be hid. Neither do men light a candle and put it under a bushel, but on a candlestick; and it giveth light unto all that are in the house. Let your light so shine before men, that they may see your good works, and glorify your father which is in heaven. Matthew 5: 13-16

We Lutherans don't have the same relationship with saints, but I do believe they represent ideals to strive for. Saint Katherine remains my favorite. The idea that one should perform the meager tasks without complaining, to see what needs to be done and do it as a form of worship without measuring whether it is "beneath you." I like this philosophy.

Humility in work is not my strong suit. I tend to throw myself into tasks with persistence and drive, whether in my professional or service endeavors, but my attitude is different from Saint Katherine's, not as pure. Fortunately, the world needs different people with different talents, and we are not all saints—that's for sure. I work hard and I tend to expect success and recognition from what I do. In fact, I'd never gotten over the nagging shame that I'd let the FBI beat me when I quit.

The reason I left was that after nearly thirteen years on duty, I realized it would be more harmful to my psyche to continue to work there than to change careers. It simply was no longer worth the price I was paying in daily humiliation. I knew the line between trying to work through a problem on the job and accepting abuse in a hostile work environment had been long ago crossed and that no amount of fighting the system was going to change that. In my heart, I knew I had made the right decision, but in the almost fourteen years since I'd left the Bureau, I had not been able to resolve my feelings of inadequacy. The truth is that what you know intellectually has little bearing upon your emotions and, somehow, my identity as a person had gotten mixed up in my identity as an FBI agent. In Kolkata I realized that the prestige of being one of the first women in the history of the FBI to work her way into supervisory ranks was meaningless in the grand scheme of the world. In fact, the time I'd spent with my patients at home and at *Kalighat* had been infinitely more significant. What had meant nothing to the world had meant the world to each of those patients and to me.

I had always told myself I'd made the right choice. At last I had no doubts. I'd been holding out in the FBI because of pride and tenacity, not because I saw the work as being of great value to mankind. After all this time, after years of explaining to people why I had left that job, I was able to see it for what it was—a job. I was able to forgive myself.

After church, I walked down the street past the boy who slept on the sidewalk near my hotel. He did not stir as I hurried by at my Washington, D.C. pace. The traffic was the lightest I'd ever seen it. No one honked—a novel experience that left me feeling somewhat in a vacuum.

I crossed the street and, keeping my eyes glued to the ground, rushed past the men who were hanging out in front of the mosque. The lowered eyes had become a reflex, a concession I made to my fear of being molested. This was not at all my normal behavior on the street, as I have always preferred to look people in the eye and greet them as I walk along.

I sat on the steps of the Mother House. Mass had not yet ended, and the redwood-brown doors with the plain wooden cross were locked to protect the contemplative atmosphere inside. The sound of sisters' singing wafted through the windows. Now, more than ever, I was struck by the oneness of their voices. No one was trying to show off their talent, to be heard above the others. One voice, one accent. Unity of purpose and faith.

When I finally got into the Mother House, there was a huge wooden rosary adorning Mother's tomb. The beads were painted like Slavic Easter eggs, the main color being the shade of blue worn by the Missionaries of Charity, with red-orange and white accents. Mother's tomb had become my cocoon against the roar and shaking of the traffic. The walls and windows blocked my view of the melee in the streets, but its sounds still managed to insinuate themselves as a far-off torrent.

As I sat in the quiet, it occurred to me that one spectacular voice cutting through the sound of a choir is not beautiful. It is discordant.

PARTING MOMENTS

I'd been crying as I said goodbye to the patients and the sisters on this, my last day at *Kalighat*. I knew it was time for me to go, but parting was still difficult.

As a farewell gift, I left a wound-care book, inscribed: "To the Missionaries of Charity (*Kalighat*) who also heal the invisible wounds. It has been a pleasure working with you." I wanted to remember to find a book on physical assessment to send once I got back to the United States.

I also donated my syringes, sutures, and needles to the dispensary. I had some shorter needles that were more appropriate for kids, so that no one else would blow out a long, skinny needle and spray medications across her face.

On this last day, I took care of several women with scabies and was having a psychosomatic response: I was itching all over. Scabies is a mite infestation that is spread by contact with an infected person. It looks like trails of irritated bumps, and it itches horribly. At Mother Teresa's it was treated with unmarked lotions but did not respond immediately. No matter what treatment agent is applied, it generally takes a couple of weeks before the itching subsides, even though the infestation is quickly killed.

Mila Little, an Australian nurse of Croatian origin whose name means "dear" in Croatian, asked me this morning whether I'd seen the woman with the worms. The woman had produced a bedpan full of big fat worms in feces. Mila said she'd never seen anything like it. She said they were not tapeworms, and the entire tangle of them was still alive. She then told me to be sure to see the next one. Yes, this is what nurses do for a good time.

My big worry of that last shift was Malti, the Marithi girl, who had pain under the ribs of her left side. She had been losing weight and nothing we did seemed to help. She'd been on antibiotics, but that was because of a respiratory problem. She described her pain by hooking her fingers under the left ribs and saying she was not feeling better. I wasn't sure what the problem was. It could have been the spleen, which is the largest lymph gland. The area she pointed to was too high for bowel, and while she had described something that could have been pleuritic pain before, I didn't think she was talking about her lungs that day. When I left Malti, I suspected that her condition would be one of those loose ends that would bother me for the rest of my life.

Later that day, I was sitting at the feet of Mother's statue, thinking of the poor woman with the worms, when I realized that parasites of various sorts could lodge anywhere—for example, visceral leishmaniasis can affect the spleen. Maybe that was Malti's problem. Fortunately, I ran into Susan and asked her to check out Malti in the morning and order whatever tests might help. I also emailed Carolyn. Maybe they could solve this problem.

Other long-term volunteers were leaving too, and I could see their behavior transitioning back to the lives they came from. That afternoon, the infamous dark humor of nursing had appeared. Kshama was waving her bandaged, putrid arm around, and a couple of nurses tried to get the rest of the women on the ward to start a stadium wave. When I saw the nurses joining together, I realized that we had made the journey from Western nurses in our safely structured environments to volunteers in this peaceful home of chaos, and that we were once again assuming our Western ways.

Mila was a metaphor for us all. She had been terribly timid about crossing in front of cars when she first arrived. Now she charged ahead of the rest of us as we made our way to *Kalighat*. When we first met, she detested the traffic. Now she stepped out as if she'd done it all her life. We had all learned a sort of defensive walking, knowing that when you make your move in Kolkata, you'd better make it fast. But what was most significant was that we'd all grown a little braver, a little more independent. And we would return to our lives a lot stronger.

Kolkata had given me many gifts in my perspective on life, as well as nursing. The United States is in the midst of a nursing crisis, and overburdened healthcare workers know that patients are the big losers in the situation. Also, people who go into the caring professions do so out of a sense of commitment. They are not satisfied with giving halfway; therefore, job satisfaction is down. This was a huge factor in my decision to leave.

The "business" of nursing has become the primary focus, and I had left business to become a nurse. What I found were moneymaking concepts superimposed upon healthcare without full regard for patient safety. "Work smarter" is a viable concept when the consequence of mistakes involves money instead of lives. In nursing, "work smarter" translates to fewer nurses and fewer assistants carrying a higher load of sicker patients, using fewer supplies. What's so smart about that?

There are tasks of nursing that by law cannot be delegated to aides: physical assessments; charting; and medication administration, which includes double-checking the appropriateness and accuracy of medications prescribed by the doctor, as well as those received from the pharmacy. For example, the nurse's legal responsibility before giving a medication is to check for side effects as they relate to the patient's condition and other medications, then to calculate the appropriate dosage. If something doesn't seem correct, it is the nurse's responsibility to question the doctor or pharmacy. The bottom line is: if the doctor orders the wrong medicine, the pharmacy fills it, and the nurse gives it, the nurse is liable.

In the litigious United States, nurses must document every patient as if a prosecutor were going to read it; take care of the multiple machines that monitor vital signs, perform dialysis, and provide ventilation; administer medications and blood; and perform physical assessments up to once an hour, depending on how sick the patient is—even every five minutes with a critical patient in an ICU. The nurse must also make sure that each patient is charged for every supply used in his care. Because of all this and the nursing shortage, most nurses work overtime—hospitals even force nurses to work mandatory overtime. The result is that nurses are too exhausted and stressed to feel that their practice is always safe. Most of us became nurses for no other reason than to provide the best possible care to others, and what I've just described isn't it. It's scary—I'd rather face a man with a gun any day than go back on that ICU floor.

The statistical trends for healing the nursing shortage aren't encouraging. According to the National Council of State Boards of Nursing in 1995, 96,438 graduates sat for the nursing board exam. In 2003, only 76,618 did. This, when in February 2004, the U.S. Bureau of Labor Statistics predicted that the United States will need more than one million new and replacement nurses by 2012. Also, in July 2001, the Government Accounting Office report, *Nursing Workforce: Emerging Nurse Shortages Due to Multiple Factors* (GAO-01-944), forecasted that forty percent of RNs will be older than age fifty by 2010, just when the baby-boomer generation will become the largest geriatrics population in U.S. history.

Studies show that on the average hospital floor nurses spend only minutes a day in personal contact with each patient. Think about the implications for patients. The average doctor rounds on hospital floors once a day or less and spends the bulk of his or her time in the office. That means they see a patient a few minutes during rounds and rely upon the nurses to identify the early stages of crises for the rest of the time. Since only a doctor or a nurse can conduct a physical assessment—which includes, for example, listening to the lungs and heart and evaluating neurological status. Doesn't it sound like a good idea to ensure nurses spend the bulk of the shift interacting with patients? Frankly, I'd rather be less high-tech and provide more personal contact.

Medical personnel tend to know from the look of the patient when a crisis is developing—for example, from skin tone, mental status, color of urine, lack of urine, the look in the eyes, or the sound of the voice. In critical patients, you often know what's going on before you lay your stethoscope on their chests because you can see, hear, or smell the problem. The key to doing this is that you need to have enough contact to catch the cues. One of the more surprising realizations of *Kalighat* is that the open wards provide that ability, even though the patient load was impossible if you just considered numbers.

My thoughts on the primitive conditions in the *Kalighat* facility had changed since my initial impression. I was beginning to understand that some of the very things I thought were necessary to provide good nursing care work against us in the United States. Take the open wards: In America, open wards are rare, if they still exist at all. Patients have private or semi-private rooms, and healthcare workers are so busy with the thousand tasks that have become a part of advanced technological care that healthcare workers are almost invisible to their charges. One of the mirthful expressions we used to say at the end of a busy nursing shift was: "All I could do was flip 'em, stick 'em, and run." Meanwhile, the patients lie in secluded rooms, thinking they are better off for their privacy, yet craving human contact to help them through the trauma of illness and injury.

Mother Teresa's was as different as it was distant from the world-fa-mous research hospitals where I trained and worked. Yet it was there that I gained a new understanding of how humans heal. The sisters and volun-teers provide respect and almost constant human contact, along with bal-anced nutrition, in a clean, though spartan environment. And with these simple measures, they heal broken bodies and spirits.

Back in my room at the Circular, late-afternoon Muslim prayers rang out. It was a haunting sound, with several mosques calling the faithful to prayer at once. They didn't seem to be saying the same thing, however. Knowing nothing about their prayers or language, I remained at a loss as to what they were saying, but I'd come to enjoy listening to it.

I had also come to realize that there was reason obscured in Kolkata's whirlpool of activity, but it was hard to see through Western eyes. From my window I heard snippets of life. It was through this opening that the muezzin called the Muslim faithful to prayer, the horns honked, goats bleated, and life was played out on the streets and sidewalks below.

I had just finished packing everything I could before morning and had settled onto the bed to watch a televised elephant polo game, when there was a knock at my door. I answered it and found one of the waiters outside.

Amal was over six feet tall, with thick black hair and mustache, slen-der but strong-looking. He was always smiling, and when he served my food, he always said, "Yes" holding the "s" extra long until it was a bit of a hiss.

He appeared to be in his thirties, and when I first met him, he had said, "Oh, you're back." Some of the sisters had reacted the same way, so I must have a twin somewhere.

Anyway, Amal asked to come in. As much as I'd liked him over the course of my visit, alarm shot through me as he closed the door behind himself. Smiling, he pushed a folded newspaper toward me, announcing, "This is for you."

I opened it tenuously, concerned I'd find some sort of contraband or something he wanted me to take on the plane with me for someone in the United States. As I peeled back the pages, I found five pictures he had painted of Christ and Mother Teresa. He asked me not to tell anyone of the gift. He was talented. Very. What a lovely surprise. He asked whether I'd be back the next year and said he'd do something larger for me.

I was knocked back by the gift. They were scrupulously detailed paintings that must have taken weeks to complete, because Amal had no electricity and could only paint a couple of hours a day.

He wore a Miraculous Medal, as did several of the Circular's waiters. Mother Teresa had once visited the Circular Hotel restaurant to see a woman who had heart trouble. The waiters offered Mother food and drink, but she wouldn't take anything for herself, saying, "Please give it to the poor." The waiters all remembered that visit.

After delivering his gifts, Amal left me with a handshake. I was ashamed that my initial reaction to having him in my room was one of fear. Then, as I studied the beautiful pictures he had given me on this, my last night at the Circular, a disturbing sound came from the street—the rhythmic chant that was characteristic of the protests in the Middle East. I couldn't see the men, but there was a crowd of excited, angry-sounding male voices drawing nearer and nearer. Since the Circular Hotel housed mostly Westerners, I started to worry. Suddenly, I didn't feel safe. Fearing a bomb blast, I drew the thick blackout curtains shut and looked around the room for the place that looked most sturdy. For once, I was glad my room was in the back of the hotel and lacking a scenic view of the street.

The voices reached a crescendo outside the blackout curtains, but by the time I decided that dragging my mattress into the bathroom would be the safest way to protect myself in a bomb blast, the violence of the chanting voices peaked and was moving away, so I stayed on my bed until the goose-call honks of vehicles and grinding of gears were the only sounds that broke the silence. Never had I felt more a foreigner in a land I did not understand.

In the morning, I returned to the Oberoi. After all the excitement, my return to the world of privilege for my last two nights seemed apropos. During my first stay, the hotel had been impressive with its opulent marble, carved wood, sweeping staircases, and enormous chandeliers, but this time around, I actually appreciated it. Everything was polished and primped, and fresh flowers bedecked the rooms and dining tables.

The writing desk in my room was my favorite part of the hotel. Its lines and little compartments for pens, ink, stamps, and stationery were reminiscent of a bygone era. There was an intricate properness to the set-up that called to mind images of Kipling and prim colonial women.

The hotel had even provided a jasmine-scented candle that added to the atmosphere. The place was heaven. My Kolkata experience, however, reminded me that the splendor of the British Empire was for the colonials, and none but few Indians were allowed to partake, except as servants standing in the wings. I suppose this contributed to their apathy in seeing the city's architecture fall to disrepair. Still, the colonial vestiges of cricket, the polo club, thoroughbred horse races, and this lovely hotel thrived.

Almost as soon as I arrived at the Oberoi Grand that morning, I went for spa services: a steam, ginger body scrub, massage, facial, and rose petal bath. It was flat-out amazing. This tiny Thai woman had the strongest hands I'd ever felt. The massage was the best I'd ever experienced, and I was euphoric by the time it was over. I don't think I'd ever felt so refreshed or clean in my life, so I scheduled more of the same for the next day.

Back in my room I put on the fluffy white robe provided by the hotel and gazed out over an expansive garden, complete with lily ponds in huge terracotta pots. In this cloistered palace there was tranquility. Tiny brown birds speckled the bushes in the garden, chirping happily, if persistently. There were no crows and, astonishingly, no honking. The central air removed humidity and flattened my frail, flimsy hair, and I awaited my appointments at the spa by sitting at the writing desk and jotting down my thoughts about my Kolkata experience.

Oddly, I missed the noise and the life teeming in the streets. There was intimacy in walking through people's lives as they bathed, shaved, argued, begged, and urinated on the streets. Vile though it was at times, I had become a part of that which had intimidated me at first. The rhythm of life was inescapable when played out in the open air: birth, death, cruelty, aging, laughter, family. Romantic love was harder to see, due to customs of morality. Love between a man and a woman was not for public display; rather for the secret chambers of alleys or behind the thick, black industrial rubber sheeting that formed the rudimentary tents where families lived.

I, however, was back in the wealthy section that boasted the New Market, where anything could be bought—I'd even seen weapons. It was time to dress and brave the realm of the "market boys" one more time to buy what I hoped would be memorable gifts to give to family and friends back home.

The market boys were licensed by the city to direct people to vendors and help them navigate the dimly lit catacombs of stalls that spilled out from the walls and into the narrow walkways. Market boys were, however, aggressive predators, especially when they spotted a Westerner. They followed me, despite my pleadings. At every step, they pleaded with me to reveal what I wanted to buy. The only reason I even considered returning to that throng was to finish Christmas shopping. I knew I'd regret it if I went back to the United States empty-handed.

"I'm only here to look," "I'm not buying today," "I hate being followed," and "Go away" fell on deaf ears. I tried not to meet their gaze, though I knew this would only provide a bit of comfort but would not rid me of the pariah.

The market boys' teeth were stained with betel, and their eyes were wide with drugs. They might have been licensed, but my law enforcement and nursing experience told me that beneath those well-dressed exteriors lurked dragons. Though by then I was an old hand on the streets, at New Market, I had safety concerns. I hated my American politeness. It painted a target across my back, and after half an hour, I fled the market without buying anything. On the way back to the hotel I found a Kashmiri government store where I bought some scarves, painted boxes, and Christmas ornaments. There was no haggling there, which was a relief. I also passed a used bookstore and bought reading materials for the plane. Finally, I bought a small suitcase to hold my presents and all the books I'd acquired over the month.

Back at the hotel, I sat on the balcony, reading and enjoying the view of the gardens. The skies had darkened, threatening rain all day. Kolkata was on the verge of monsoon season and, as I sat there watching, a prelude began. The drops were large and widely spaced; the weight of them was impressive when they slammed against my head and body. I didn't go in immediately because the warm, humidity-filled breeze was just as I liked it, reminding me of the shores of the Gulf of Mexico. In humidity, I always feel as if my skin fits. In dryer climes, it is just a bit too tight.

As the rain picked up, I retreated to my room and watched from the window as water suddenly dropped like a veil from heaven. The sound of it was heavy, pelting. The gutters in the garden below my balcony gushed to overflowing after only five minutes.

In the beauty of the rain that fed the verdant gardens of the Oberoi Grand Hotel, I wondered what was happening to the people who lived on the street. In the gardens of the Grand, the rain was beautiful, a true gift of nature. Though it relieved the monotony of the Kolkata hot season, I doubted that street dwellers stood transfixed as I did. But I gazed from the balcony of my lemongrass-scented room and retreated to the spa when the downpour threatened to drench me.

During my massage the next afternoon, the thunder and deluge returned. By the time I emerged in a pampered state of grace, the environs of this palace had morphed to an intensely green, sparkling world. Everything was fresh and clean. Birds cheeped as they splashed in small pools of liquid. They dipped their beaks and threw back their heads, twisting their feathered bodies and flapping their wings in the bath.

I snapped picture after picture of this wonderland. Through the wall-sized glass windows that connected the hall passages to nature streamed a wedding party. They were wearing the saris dreams are made of: ruby reds beaded with gold filigreed designs, royal blue with accents that imitated the hues of a peacock's tail. All the women were gorgeous in their bangles of gold.

Earlier that day, I'd had a conversation with a young Indian girl who had told me that my hair was beautiful, which was actually a first for me. In my mind's eye, my hair was a haystack, its gray roots in need of a dye job. I told her, in all sincerity, that I would rather have hers, which was thick and onyx-colored, drawn tightly into a chignon. She admitted it fell to her waist when loose. Because mine is curly and frail, I'd never succeeded in getting it past my shoulders. We laughed about how it was human nature to want what one could not have.

At the pool there were only the sounds of bubbling water and the small brown birds that zipped across the lawn at a speed that rivaled the mice the cats caught in our old farmhouse in Maryland. There were flowers everywhere but not the scarlet hibiscus and golden marigolds seen in the market near *Kalighat*. The sounds of the street and the incessant honking were obliterated by the towering walls of this fortress hotel. Yardmen worked silently, almost invisible among the guests.

The newspapers came, and one brought me back to reality. *The Telegraph*

Calcutta's headlines read, "Crash children lie in neglect, families seethe." The article said that twenty-six children had been admitted to the hospital after a passenger train hit their school bus. The conditions at the hospital that drove relatives to fury included that many of the children still lay in a "stinking corridor" after a night in the hospital without food, medicine, or water. One man said: "They would not let us take our patient anywhere else for treatment. Nor would they let us procure medicines from outside. We are helpless. They are doing nothing."

True to the pattern I'd seen in each of the horror stories about Indian hospitals that month, the hospital denied that conditions were bad. Hospital spokesman Ganesh Saha pooh-poohed charges with the comment, "No written complaint has come to me yet. What you are talking about?"

The story ended with relatives taking matters into their own hands and chasing Saha down a corridor. Saha managed to make it to his office, where he locked the door from the inside.[44]

Once again, I could not resolve the contrast of beauty and pain in this horrible, magical land. It was time for me to leave.

A TALE OF TWO CITIES

Just one degree south of the Tropic of Cancer, Kolkata arose from three villages near the banks of the Hugli River. The city, once a thriving port and the capital of British India, now occupies both sides of the Gangetic tributary; but navigating the river these days is made treacherous by sandbars and perpetual deposits of silt. Only daily dredging keeps the port viable. While no longer the capital of India, Kolkata is the capital of West Bengal, and its jungle is now of the concrete variety.

My home is a historic house in rural Maryland, relatively near Washington, D.C. J.E.B. Stuart slept there on his way to Gettysburg, and it was built by the Hood family whose famous relative—and mine—is General John Bell Hood. The fact that Hood lost more men than any other general in the Confederacy belies the peace of this place, where the air is clean and gentle washing up from the cornfields and over the gardens where daffodils, iris, crocus, tulips, and hyacinths color the beds and peek from between the forest-green and periwinkle of the vincas. Rose bushes line the white picket fence, and azaleas, rhododendrons, and giant forsythias brighten the back acreage. The only smell is the freshness of new-mown grass. There is no sand, no crowds of people. It is pristine and safe.

I can sit on my kitchen porch and see no one, not even another house. There are only fields, forested hills, and a few barns. The sounds I hear are made by the breeze jostling leaves, and a variety of birds, who are vibrant this spring, perhaps because of the appearance of cicadas, which only emerge every seventeen years.

Our water comes from a well, and has been tested as pure ever since we've lived here. Our well never runs dry, since it was built to accommodate herds of dairy cows. Before I went to Kolkata, I took this for granted. It never occurred to me that clean water might not be there when I opened the tap or that any city's water might contain sewage or arsenic.

Deer wander near the house in the evenings, more bold than I'd imagined before living here. And fat, sassy squirrels race across the lawn, tormenting the cats. While they are impressive mousers, the cats have never succeeded in catching these squirrels.

As night falls, I look to the heavens where stars crowd the skies like diamonds on velvet. There is none of the "light pollution" that blocks sky views in cities, nor is there pollution of any kind. It is perfect for evenings with my telescope. Kolkata nights seemed perpetually occluded by clouds, and only a few of the brightest objects in the sky were able to shine through. This was a disappointment, as I had wanted to stargaze near the Tropic of Cancer.

I don't comprehend the discrepancies in the way I live and the lives of so many others on earth. I don't even know how to think of this. It seems too simple to say "life ain't fair" or "it's God's will." I watch a nest of barn swallows, beautiful birds that have taken up residence under the eaves of my front porch. Our cats will kill some of their babies this year, and I know this is the order of things. Simplistic as it is, this is probably the answer to my question, but it is not an answer I can accept. For me the search continues.

I'm back at my job at the Department of Defense. There's a war on and we're busy. My son faces yet another deployment, despite the fact that his wife will give birth in a couple of months to their second son. My daughter is ill and has been in and out of the hospital, so I'm glad I am here for her now. And I still fall prey to ire over life's little problems, but when I take the time to stop and reflect, the memories of Kolkata renew me.

I'm so busy that at times Kolkata seems long ago and far away, but today I received email from Carolyn, saying she will be in Kolkata in January. Could I come?

Mother Teresa said:

Stay where you are. Find your own Calcutta. Find the sick, the suffering and the lonely right there where you are—in your own homes and in your own families, in your workplaces and in your schools…You can find Calcutta all over the world, if you have the eyes to see. Everywhere, wherever you go, you find people who are unwanted, unloved, uncared-for, just rejected by society—completely forgotten, completely left alone.[45]

I know she's right. I mean, who could argue with Mother Teresa? These days, I volunteer at her Baltimore AIDS hospice, but oh, how I long for Kolkata.

I remember my last day at the Circular, saying goodbye to the waiters. I was surprised at how hard this was. They had become my friends, and as the doorman and cab driver were wrestling my book-filled bags into the taxi, I ran into an Italian man I'd been working with. He didn't speak much English, but his English was better than my Italian. He took my hand.

"Going?" he asked.

"Yes," I said, "until the next time."

"Oh," he shook his head, still holding my hand, "*Kalighat*." He shrugged as if to say, "What will *Kalighat* do without you?"

I smiled and said, "Thank you for your work," and I know that because of people like him, and of course the sisters, *Kalighat* and the other work of the Missionaries of Charity will go on long after each of us as individuals has ceased to be.

The spiritual realization of my trip was coming to understand why it is a privilege to serve others. "It's more blessed to give than receive" implies it is a gift to be the helper, rather than one who needs help. But there is more: when you give of yourself, what you get back is hope. With hope you can get through tough times, and it is hope that makes life worth living.

For me, the Missionaries of Charity have inspired a lifetime quest. Because of them, the month in Kolkata is not the end of my story but the beginning of a new way of life. My goals are set: I will serve the poor in my own country, and when I can, I will travel to foreign lands and be a nurse to people no one wants. My rewards have already been more than I imagined: new friends across the world, memories that bring smiles, and peace that passes understanding.

I remain a Lutheran but am privileged to attend mass with the Missionaries of Charity in Baltimore and to work alongside them. The Missionaries are the kindest, most innocent people I've ever met. They have taught me to take joy in simple things, and I feel good just being around them. As I look to my future through the eyes Mother Teresa and her followers gave me, I can't wait to see tomorrow.

ENDNOTES

[1] Scott Baldauf, "India's bid to boost healthcare in slums," *The Christian Science Monitor*, May 27, 2004. Retrieved from http://www.csmonitor.com.

[2] Joan M. Teno, MD, MS; Brian R. Clarridge, PhD; Virginia Casey, PhD, MPH; Lisa C. Welch, MA; Terrie Wetle, PhD; Renee Shield, PhD; Vincent Mor, PhD, "Family Perspectives on End-of-Life Care at the Last Place of Care," *JAMA*, 2004;291:88-93. Retrieved from http://jama.ama-assn.org.

[3] Mother Teresa, Nobel lecture. Retrieved from http://www.nobel.se/peace/laureates/1979/teresa-lecture.html.

[4] Retrieved from http://www.state.gov.

[5] Chandan Nandy, "Serial thefts erode Tagore collection," *Hindustan Times*. Retrieved from http://www.hindustantimes.com.

[6] Retrieved from The Official Site of the Nobel Foundation, http://www.nobel.se/literature/laureates/1913/.

[7] Rabindranath Tagore, *Gitanjali* [Song Offerings] (verse 35), 1910. Retrieved from Allspirit at http://www.allspirit.co.uk/gitanjali.html#2.

[8] Rabindranath Tagore, *Crisis in Civilisation & Other Essays* (New Delhi: Rupa & Co., 2003) p. 14.

[9] Sarmila Maiti, "Rare succour for terminally ill: Very soon, Kolkata will

get its first hospice at Nrendrapur," *The Times of India*, Calcutta Times, p. I.

10 Saint Charles Borromeo Philippine Medical Mission, newsletter, Spring/ Summer 2003. Retrieved from http://pmm.stcharleschurch.org/docs/pm mNewsletter2003SpringSummer.pdf.

11 Mother Teresa, Nobel Lecture. Retrieved from http://www.nobel.se/ peace/laureates/1979/teresa-lecture.html.

12 Ascension Research Center, "Mother Teresa." Retrieved from http:// www.ascension-research.org/teresa.html.

13 Mother Teresa, Nobel Lecture. Retrieved from http://www.nobel.se/ peace/laureates/1979/teresa-lecture.html.

14 Retrieved from http://nobelprize.org/peace/laureates/1979/presenta- tion-speech.html.

15 Retrieved from http://www.ewtn.com/motherteresa/words.htm.

16 Address of John Paul II to the pilgrims who had come to Rome for the beatification of Mother Teresa, Monday, 20 October 2003. Retrieved from http://www.vatican.va/holy_father/john_paul_ii/speeches/2003/october/ documents/hf_jp-ii_spe_20031020_pilgrims-mother-teresa_en.html.

17 Yajnaseni Chakraborty, "Reserve Bank of India's First Home in Ruins," *Hindustan Times*, HT City Timepass, p. 7.

18 Reuters Health, "U.S. medical students to get pain course online." September 9, 2003. Retrieved from http://www.healthvision.com/.

19 Patrick Wall, *Pain: The Science of Suffering* (New York: Columbia University Press, 2000).

20 Anahad O'Connor, "Brain Scans Substantiate Feel-the-Pain Senti- ments," February 24, 2004. Retrieved from http://www.nytimes.com.

21 *The Times of India*, Kolkata, "Spurt in gastro cases, hundreds in hospital," April 13, 2004, p. 8.

22 Seddon R. Savage, "Opioid Medications in the Management of Pain," in *Principles of Addiction Medicine*, 3rd Ed, (Chevy Chase: American Society for Addiction Medicine, 2003) pp. 1453-1455.

23 Mother Teresa's speech at the National Prayer Breakfast, February 5, 1994. Retrieved from http://www.catholiceducation.org.

[24] World Health Organization, *"Factsheet N°275: Substandard and counterfeit medicines,"* November 2003, http://www.who.int/mediacentre/factsheets/2003/fs275/en/.

[25] Rajib Chakraborty, "Fake doctor arrested after child's death," *The Hindustan Times*, HT Kolkata Live, p. 19.

[26] Debashis Konar, "RS 25 LAKHS TO BE A DOC! Pay a premium to get into a medical college through a donor seat," *The Times of India*, Calcutta Times section, p. I.

[27] Government of India, The Scheduled Castes and the Scheduled Tribes (Prevention of Atrocities) Act, Section 3, September 11, 1989.

[28] Tapan Das, "SSKM withdraws free beds for arsenic patients," *Hindustan Times*, HT Kolkata Live, p. 20.

[29] *The Times of India*, "Choke-o-meter," April 16, 2004, City Life, p. 3.

[30] *The Times of India*, "Heat stroke kills one as city reels under heat wave," April 16, 2004, City Life, p. 3.

[31] *The Times of India*, "Water pollution gives rise to gastro cases," *Calcutta Times*, p. I.

[32] *The Telegraph Calcutta*, "Death rules roost, brides keep off," April 17, 2004.

[33] *The Telegraph Calcutta*, "By their own hand," Women, April 18, 2004, p. 3.

[34] *Hindustan Times*, "No place at home if either parent dislikes your wife," HT Kolkata Live, p. 19.

[35] Gurcharan Das, *The Elephant Paradigm: India Wrestles with Change* (Penguin Books, 2002).

[36] Richard E. Nisbett, *The Geography of Thought: How Asians and Westerners Think Differently ... and Why* (Free Press, 2004).

[37] Gurcharan Das, op cit, p. 239.

[38] Geoffrey Moorhouse, *Kolkata: The City Revealed* (Penguin Books India, 1994), p. 12.

[39] Gurcharan Das, op cit, p. 240.

[40] Ibid, p. 241.

[41] Ibid, p. 241.

[42] Rabindranth Tagore, *Crisis in Civilisation*, (New Delhi: Rupa & Co., 2003), p. 20.

[43] Rajib Chakrabory, "Childbirth outside hospital as doc sleeps," *Hindustan Times*, April 22, 2004, HT Kolkata Live, p. 19.

[44] Kuheli Chakravorty, "Crash children lie in neglect, families seethe," *The Telegraph Calcutta*, April 29, 2004, p. 9.

[45] Retrieved from http://www.usccb.org.